AF703369

The Shades of Aeneas

The Shades of Aeneas

The Imitation of Vergil and the History of Paganism in Boccaccio's *Filostrato*, *Filocolo*, and *Teseida*

JAMES H. MCGREGOR

The University of Georgia Press
Athens and London

© 1991 by the University of Georgia Press
Athens, Georgia 30602
All rights reserved
Designed by Mary Mendell
Set in Stempel Garamond
The paper in this book meets the guidelines for permanence and durability of the Committee on Production Guidelines for Book Longevity of the Council on Library Resources.
Printed in the United States of America

95 94 93 92 91 5 4 3 2 1

Library of Congress Cataloging in Publication Data

McGregor, James H. (James Harvey), b. 1946.
The shades of Aeneas: the imitation of Vergil and the history of paganism in Boccaccio's Filostrato, Filocolo, and Teseida / James H. McGregor.
p. cm.
Includes bibliographical references and index.
ISBN 0-8203-1301-7 (cloth: alk. paper)
1. Boccaccio, Giovanni, 1313–1375—Knowledge—History. 2. Dante Alighieri, 1265–1321—Influence—Boccaccio. 3. Virgil—Influence—Boccaccio. 4. Virgil. Aeneis. 5. Italian literature—Roman influences. 6. Imitation (in literature) 7. Paganism in literature. 8. History in literature. I. Title.
PQ4293.H5M36 1991
851'.1—dc20 90-42488
CIP

British Library Cataloging in Publication Data available

Contents

Preface

THE PORTRAIT OF BOCCACCIO that emerges from this work is a new one. I describe him here as a poet concerned with history, with the accurate depiction of details of Roman religion, with the imitation of Vergil, and ultimately with the condemnation of paganism and the exposure of its pretensions and spiritual limitations. All of these are approaches that Boccaccio shares with Dante and with the poets of the High Renaissance. None of them has been attributed to him in the past.

The three works I examine here not only share a focus on the ancient world and the imitation of Vergil but also suggest a progressive deepening of Boccaccio's engagement with the antique. *Filostrato* is the story of those who do not outlive Troy's fall. It contrasts the actions of its hero, Troilus, with those of Aeneas, and it suggests that the patterns of action that distinguish these heroes justify the differing fates of the cities they represent. The Troy of Troilus is characterized by obsessive love and disobedience to divine command. Aeneas exerts self-control and is responsive to the will of the gods, and these become the dominant characteristics of the nation he will found. *Filocolo* shows a collaboration between men and gods that leads, as the *Aeneid* leads, to the establishment by men of divinely sponsored institutions. Collaboration between men and gods is again at issue in *Teseida.* There, however, while Theseus tries to do good, he finds himself opposed by divinities who, in this instance, are covertly demonic. *Teseida* addresses the problem of paganism per se and argues for the necessity of grace in the management of human passion. From his stance as a continuator or imitator of Vergilian themes in *Filostrato,* then, Boccaccio becomes, in *Teseida,* the judge of paganism and of Vergil himself. In this role he resembles his great predecessor, Dante.

Filostrato, Filocolo, and *Teseida,* the works described here, are not familiar to many American readers, though they deserve to be. Each, in fact, has been translated into English within the last decade. *Filo-*

strato, a poem of some seven thousand stanzas, is set in the period of the Trojan War. It describes the disastrous love of Troilus and Criseida. *Filocolo* is a prose romance centering on the triumphant love of Florio and Biancifiore and the events that love brings about. *Il Teseida delle nozze d'Emilia*—to give the work its rarely used full title—is a Thesead based on Statius's first-century epic poem, the *Thebaid.* Each of these romances is set in the ancient world, and each, as this study shows, is heavily influenced by Vergil's *Aeneid.* Boccaccio wrote them between about 1334 and 1341 in his native Florentine dialect. He finished the last when he was twenty-nine years old. Some seven years later, he began the *Decameron.*

English readers who know the poems are probably aware of them as the sources for some of Chaucer's most popular works. Readers who have never read Boccaccio's *Teseida* know a great deal about it through Chaucer's "Knight's Tale." Chaucer's *Troilus and Criseyde* is an extensive imitation of Boccaccio's *Filostrato.* The "Franklin's Tale" is derived from an episode of *Filocolo,* although the main theme of the romance bears little relationship to that tale. Throughout this study, then, readers of Chaucer will frequently find echoes of what they already know. Chaucer is a tendentious imitator, however, and he uses Boccaccio's texts for his own purposes. Inevitably, then, much of what this study documents will seem strange even to Chaucerians.

While I hope this book will redefine some of the terms of comparison between Boccaccio and Chaucer by describing a side of Boccaccio that has not been clearly seen before, this study is not a comparison of the two. It concerns the classical tradition to which Boccaccio responded and the influence of Dante as literary and intellectual predecessor. Fortunately, the task of describing the tradition Boccaccio initiates with these works and his influence on Chaucer is well underway in a number of excellent studies by such scholars as Derek Brewer, Nicholas Havely, Piero Boitani, and especially David Wallace.[1] I hope that the new picture of Boccaccio introduced here, in addition to establishing the notion of Boccaccio as a serious student of Vergil, will lead to some revised notions of the interaction between Boccaccio and Chaucer as well.

The writing of this book has been sustained and supported by a variety of institutions. A first draft was completed while I was a fellow in postclassical humanistic studies at the American Academy in

Rome. My tenure there was supported by a grant from the National Endowment for the Humanities and a Sarah Moss Traveling Fellowship from the University of Georgia. I wish to express my gratitude to these institutions and especially to Sophie Consagra, then director of the American Academy in Rome. My readings of Boccaccio and Vergil have been aided by the work of many friends, including Robert Hollander, Janet Smarr, John V. Fleming, and William S. Anderson. As always, I am grateful to Sallie for her comments and support.

1

Introduction

IN AN EARLIER STUDY, I ARGUED that Boccaccio, in three of his early works, arrived at an increasingly detailed and verisimilar representation of the religious practices of the classical world.[1] My aim was to persuade the reader that pre-Christian worship was, within the limits of Boccaccio's sources and methods, carefully described and that Boccaccio's purpose for doing so was to create accurate and believable settings for his poems about antiquity. At the end of that study I posed an obvious question. If it is true that the details of pagan religious practice in *Filostrato, Filocolo,* and *Teseida* are verisimilar, what is Boccaccio's larger purpose in making them so? That question is the focus of the present study. Here I will try to show that Boccaccio's verisimilitude is not just a matter of style but is thematic and ultimately polemical. It aims to engage Roman poetry, especially Vergil, and to convince Boccaccio's reader that each of these three poems is actually about the ancient world in which it is set. Each text addresses that world and addresses the difference between the classical past and Boccaccio's Christian era. Not only is *Filostrato* set in the Troy of Aeneas, I will argue, but it is also about that city; *Filocolo* has a complex historical theme closely linked to that of the *Aeneid;* and *Teseida* rigorously examines and judges important aspects of pre-Christian culture as Vergil presents them.

While it might seem likely, if not obvious, that a poem set in Troy is actually about Troy or, more generally speaking, that poems set in the ancient world are actually about the world of their setting, this has not been the opinion of scholars who have examined Boccaccio. The majority have refused to ascribe any historical intention to Boccaccio or to credit him with success in rendering the ancient world as distinct from his contemporary one. Almost all of Boccaccio's critics have held that his romances are set in thinly disguised versions of the Naples and Florence of his own day.[2]

A number of factors have contributed to this negative view. In

Boccaccio's oeuvre itself, these poems are granted a secondary position. They were written almost entirely in Naples between about 1334 and 1341. Boccaccio was no older than twenty-nine when he completed them and was about seven years away from beginning his great vernacular work, the *Decameron*.[3] Grouped with others under the pejorative title of *opere minori*, these poems are generally regarded as juvenile and of interest primarily as records of Boccaccio's stylistic development. Naples, too, with its Angevin court, seems to many a retrograde force in trecento culture.[4] Boccaccio is often credited with literary seriousness only after he returned to Florence in 1341.

These views are readily contradicted by the abundant evidence of Boccaccio's erudite activity in his Neapolitan period. Late in the thirties he appears to have begun translations of Valerius Maximus's *Facta et dicta memorabilia* and books 20 through 39 of Livy's history of Rome. In one of Boccaccio's own notebooks, one reflecting the researches of this period, there is a series of excerpts representing the course of Roman and European history from the late republican period to the thirteenth century.[5] The text includes passages from Caesar, Suetonius, Orosius, Eusebius, and others. Another notebook records his interest in Latin poetry: it includes the unique copy of Dante's exchange of literary eclogues with Giovanni del Virgilio and a number of Latin poems, including one based on a Roman sepulchral inscription.[6]

Extrinsic factors have their role in diverting attention away from Boccaccio's accomplishments in these works. The romance genre, to which each of the three belongs, is often regarded as incapable of high seriousness. Classicizing romances in other languages both before and after Boccaccio's time have been viewed in terms analogous to those that have characterized Boccaccio criticism. Writers examining the French romances of antiquity have not generally found historical verisimilitude in them.[7] Even the great contemporary of Boccaccio, Francesco Petrarca, despite his obvious historical intent in the *Africa*, has been seen as incapable of distinguishing the truly historical from the anachronistic.[8]

A single general conception probably underlies this negative assessment of pre-Renaissance classicism. The historical consciousness of these medieval and early Renaissance writers has been denied a priori by a theory that still holds sway among literary historians. According to this widely held view, the men of the Middle Ages saw themselves as the continuators of classical culture. The Renaissance imagined itself as cut off from this past. It was only after the invention of the Dark Ages as a historical period intervening between the fall of classical culture and its Renaissance rediscovery that any view of the past as past could be maintained. Since pre-Renaissance men had no notion of a period in which classical culture died out and something new began, this theory argues, they could not see themselves as distinct from antiquity.

This view, despite its crudeness, does reflect a truth about Renaissance historicism and about the bent of the Renaissance in general. It was the particular triumph of the Renaissance to come to some recognition of style as an observable aspect of a work of art and as one with historical associations and limitations. Writers of the Renaissance began to be able to discriminate between objects produced in various large historical periods—classical, Gothic, Renaissance—on the basis of style. Since stylistic discrimination has proved a powerful tool right up to the present moment, this Renaissance discovery is still given great importance. Boccaccio did not use stylistic tools to distinguish his own era from that of the ancients, yet he knew perfectly well that he lived in a world completely different from theirs. For him the decisive difference was made by the fundamental change in human history represented by the Incarnation. That watershed event decisively separated classical and Christian culture, and for a poet attuned to the differences in content, if not in style, between Christian and pagan thought, that event could become a powerful principle of discrimination.

Before the Incarnation the world was pagan—after it, Christian. This decisive change, however, did not mean that Christian principles were inapplicable to the world before Christ. The Christian God governed and Providence was active, but pagan men were ignorant of the true order of history and cosmology. In such historical reasoning, Boccaccio reflects the thinking of Paulus Orosius, a Christian apologist whose *Septem libri historiarum adversum paganos* was written in the early fifth century. Orosius was popular and influential throughout the Middle Ages, and Boccaccio copied portions of his text in his *Zibaldone Magliabechiano.* Orosius, as Robert Hanning has observed, "constructed a Roman 'history of salvation,' modelled on that of the biblical Israel, but with Roman events and development as its central concern."[9]

Boccaccio, like many medieval writers before him, saw the major events of Roman history—the founding by Aeneas, the destruction of Carthage, the consolidation of the empire under Augustus—in Orosian terms. They understood these events as part of God's providential plan to establish Christianity as a universal religion with Rome as its seat. Not all events of the pagan past, however, had such positive associations. In general terms, once Boccaccio established a mode for depicting his characters and settings as Roman and pagan, the Orosian historical viewpoint permitted him to judge that past and discriminate those aspects of individual and social life that were in tune or in discord with this providential development. Such judgments form the basis of his critique of classical culture.

This judgmental role, which Boccaccio shares with Dante, is itself Orosian: "The role of Rome in the divine scheme is that of a chosen nation progressing towards Christ, and finally enjoying triumphant union with the Church; and the continuous process of divine judgment passed figurally on man (especially on sinners) is everywhere apparent in the history of Rome."[10] While Boccaccio discriminates the pagan past from the present by carefully reconstructing its religious practices, then, he judges it in Christian terms. The pagan world may be analogous to the Christian or biblical world, but it is always separate from that world.

The Orosian historical viewpoint that Boccaccio makes his own is derived from the celebratory, progressive historiography of the Augustan era. For Orosius, as for literary history itself, this view is best represented in Vergil. The *Aeneid* establishes the Augustan empire as the divinely destined final cause of Rome's founding. Christian apologists had little difficulty extending this view into their own era by replacing Vergil's endpoint with the Incarnation. As a representative of the pagan historical view as well as the major repository of classical Latin culture, then, Vergil is primary. Boccaccio, as we will see, is as devoted to him as are Augustine, Orosius, or perhaps even Dante.

In reading Vergil, Boccaccio appears to follow the pattern of Dante's *Commedia.* There the *Aeneid* is clearly seen in Orosian terms.[11] In insisting on a fundamental divide between paganism and Christianity, Boccaccio may also be guided by Dante's continued exposure of the limitations of Vergil's vision, itself a fundamental theme of the *Commedia.* In his recent study, *Il Virgilio dantesco: Tragedia nella "Commedia,"* Robert Hollander has assessed Dante's double image of his great predecessor and fictional guide.[12] Hollander extends and clarifies Paul Renucci's suggestive notion that Dante is both the "disciple" and "judge" of Vergil.[13] Dante imitates the *Aeneid*, then, but he exposes its shortcomings as well; and Hollander sees this dual process at work in Dante's enforcement of a generic distinction between himself and Vergil. Vergil is the poet of tragedy, but Dante is the poet of comedy. What is crucial here is not style but content. In the last analysis the factor that critically divides the two poets is faith. Dante is the Christian poet whose poem is triumphant, hopeful, and joyous in its conclusion. Vergil is the pagan poet gifted with only a partial vision of truth and convinced of the tragic limitation of human action. Hollander's view is undoubtedly correct: Dante views Vergil as a great but limited predecessor. He is admired for his complex vision, but "it is nonetheless true that Vergil is condemned in his work as a pagan."[14]

The most persistent, loving, and perspicacious reader of Dante was, without doubt, Giovanni Boccaccio. Throughout his life he imitated Dante, edited his works, and commented on them. What has not been remarked, however, is the degree to which Boccaccio, perhaps in imitation of Dante, modeled his own works on those of Vergil. In what follows, I will document, in most cases for the first time, Boccaccio's systematic turning to Vergil as a source not just for incidental detail but also for themes and structural foundations in three of his early works. Boccaccio's view of Vergil finally emerges as quite close to Dante's own as Hollander has described it. Throughout Boccaccio's work, Vergil is a pagan poet with pagan strengths and subject to pagan limitations. First and foremost, he is the poet of Roman destiny. In describing this very destiny, however, he fails to perceive the Christian and providential purpose that governs and shapes it.

Only one of Boccaccio's works directly addresses the *Aeneid* and discusses its interpretation. Boccaccio began his *Genealogie deorum gentilium* in about 1351, almost a decade after the completion of the last of the works I discuss here. In its fourteenth chapter, he discusses Vergil's purposes in writing the poem. The imitation of Homer is primary; praise of the Julian family and glorification of Rome are also significant parts of the poem, in his view. The only issue of interpretation raised concerns the love of Dido and Aeneas. According to Boccaccio, Vergil "represents in Dido the attracting power of the passion of love, prepared for every opportunity, and in Aeneas one who is readily disposed in that way and at length overcome. But after showing the enticements of lust, he points the way of return to virtue by bringing in Mercury, messenger of the gods, to rebuke Aeneas, and call him back from such indulgence to deeds of glory."[15] The main concern of this reading is passion and the way passion is overcome. For Boccaccio this is the major problem not only of the *Aeneid* but also of each of his romances engaging Vergil's poem. In all three, characters are confronted with the problem of managing and mastering their emotions.

In medieval literature the control of the passions is the proper subject of moral or tropological allegory. In its concentration on timeless human problems, allegory of this kind easily excludes history, and moral allegory often ignores broader spiritual issues. In Boccaccio's treatment, however, we see a continual engagement among history, allegory, and spirituality. Boccaccio will ultimately show that it is only Christianity that, through the satisfaction of man's original sin, makes possible the management of passion. While he maintains that Aeneas's response to the passion he feels for Dido is the prototypical issue in Vergil's poetry, he will ultimately reject not just the power of Vergil but the power of pagan society to respond effectively to that central concern.

While Vergil is not explicitly mentioned in any of the works I am describing, his presence is apparent in each. A handful of Vergilian episodes are referred to again and again. They were the most popular and best known in Boccaccio's day, and they remain so in our own. As I have already suggested, the love of Dido and Aeneas is central to Boccaccio's understanding of Vergil's poem. Similarly, the hero's continued battle to dominate those aspects of his personality that inhibit his divine mission is continually referred to. The providential plan in history is equally important; it sees Aeneas as the founder of the city not only destined for *imperium,* but destined, too, in Orosius's view, to be converted to Christianity and to serve as the center of Christ's earthly kingdom.

Filostrato is centered in Troy in the period that precedes the Greek victory.[16] This is the time described by the *Iliad*, a poem about which Boccaccio and his generation knew almost nothing. It is a crucial period for Aeneas, however, and it is fully described in the second book of the *Aeneid.* I will argue that Boccaccio's aim in *Filostrato* is to adumbrate the theme of the *Aeneid* by contrasting the fate of those who escape Troy with Aeneas with the fate of those who perish in the doomed city. Boccaccio answers, I will argue, a theodicean question also raised by the *Aeneid:* what justifies the divine destruction of Troy? Boccaccio finds the answer to that question in terms different from Vergil's, but in terms derived from his poem. Troilus's abuse of love and his disobedience to divine command distinguish him from Aeneas and determine his fate and that of the city he exemplifies.

The Vergilian presence in *Filocolo* is even more marked.[17] Vergil's providential view of Roman history as Christianized by Orosius is the thematic base of Boccaccio's story. He uses the lovers, Florio and Biancifiore, as he uses Troilus—as heroes around whom larger historical issues are focused. In the pattern of their love he finds the motive in the lives of individuals for the providential action of history. Boccaccio's *Teseida* is based on Statius's *Thebaid,* but the major characters in the poem are, as I will show, metaphorically identified with characters in the *Aeneid.*[18] *Teseida* records the failure of Theseus to exert the kind of control over his own actions that Aeneas, aided by the gods and his own *pietas,* frequently, although not always, achieves.

Boccaccio's verisimilar representation of pagan religious practices, then, has a thematic purpose. It prepares the way for a reassessment, in specifically Christian terms, of pagan culture. While insisting on the crucial divide that separates pagan and Christian, Boccaccio brings to bear the universal truths of Christian revelation as a superior form of explanation. He both represents and judges the pagan world and the works that describe it. He presents to his Christian reader a world that is historically past but still vital in its ability to illustrate the fundamental forces in history and human nature which he believes Christianity, in a manner excelling pagan philosophy, has discerned.

2

Filostrato

"De' Troian L'Amor Fallace"

FILOSTRATO IS THE STORY OF A young hero whom love destroys. Troilus's story is timeless; the choice he makes could be made by a man of any era. Boccaccio's narrator emphasizes the timelessness of the story and its relevance to his own age by an analogy: the love of Troilus, he says in the dedication, is like his own love for Filomena.[1] Neither this analogy, however, nor the intrinsic timelessness of the story cancels the historical situation of the romance. Troilus may act like Everyman; he may seem to be a personification of the concupiscible and irascible passions. Nevertheless, he is called Troilus, and his story is set in a city well known to history and legend at its moment of crisis.

Critics of the poem have ignored this historical setting. The "autobiographical" critics of the early part of this century saw Filostrato, the narrative persona here, as one more of Boccaccio's thinly veiled self-representations.[2] For them, the story was a roman à clef, and its "dedicatee," Filomena, stood for one of Boccaccio's own early loves. Even scholars who have rejected biographical criticism have not done away with the analysis of the poem in such intentional terms.[3] Until recently, little consideration has been given to the meaning of the text in and of itself.[4] The most penetrating analysis of *Filostrato* is Robert Hollander's *Boccaccio's Two Venuses.* Hollander's is an allegorical reading of *Filostrato;* he focuses on Troilus's choice of an unworthy love and the death to which it leads him. While I agree with Hollander's ultimate view of Troilus's choice, my aim is to add to his reading a dimension that has been neglected but that I feel is intrinsic to the poem. My reading aims to make sense not only of its theme or allegory but also of its historical setting.

None of the critical approaches I have alluded to above is able to answer the question "Why Troilus, why Troy?"[5] A fictional autobiography or compensatory myth could be set anywhere from Troy to Baghdad. An allegory of the martial and libidinal passions, such as Hollander sees in the poem, is similarly capable of any number of expressions. From the point of view of each of these critical stances, Troy and the character of Troilus are simply accidents. They will do, but many others would have done as well. Such an ahistorical viewpoint ignores the care with which Boccaccio has worked his Trojan setting and the theme of the Trojan War into the structure of *Filostrato*. It will be the aim of the first part of this chapter, then, to show that not only are characters in the Troy legend the main actors in *Filostrato* but events of the war figure in the story as well. They do not figure as mere background: Boccaccio has carefully joined the events of the Troy legend with the love story of Troilus and Criseida. Those events interfere directly in the course of their affair, and the theme of their love and the history of the war interact continually.[6]

The first event in *Filostrato* is the defection of the prophet Calchas from the Trojan to the Greek camp. This defection serves as the spring to the decisive action of the poem, since Calchas is Criseida's father and he is eventually able to win her from Troy, too. When she leaves the city, she begins to forget her Trojan lover, Troilus. His response is suicidal. Calchas's defection, then, is, long before the fact, the first link in the chain that leads to Troilus's death. Calchas's motivation for leaving Troy is clear. He leaves because he sees, thanks to the gods' gift of prophecy, a vision of "the Trojans dead, and their land destroyed" (*Filos.* 1.8.7–8). As readers, we know his vision to be correct; and, while we may not applaud his decision to join his country's enemies, his departure from Troy is like the later abandonment by the more honorable and unwilling Aeneas.

This initial action is quickly reinforced by the second scene, in which love for Criseida begins to be kindled in Troilus.[7] The two meet and fall in love in the temple of Pallas, where the goddess is venerated in the form of an image called the Palladium. This temple is an excellent thematic focus for the initiation of love between Troilus and Criseida, since the Palladium, as Vergil describes, is the key to Troy's fall. While it remains in Troy, the city is invulnerable.[8] When Ulysses and Diomedes succeed in carrying it off to the Greek camp, the city is doomed. Boccaccio recalls that doom most directly when he refers to the image, in a phrase borrowed from Vergil, as "Palladio fatale" (*Filos.* 1.18.4). This fatal and fateful Palladium presides over the scene of love's beginning for Troilus and Criseida and is as pregnant with images of doom for them as it is for Troy.

If Calchas had not left Troy beforehand, his daughter would not have been forced to follow. If Troilus and Criseida had not fallen in love, her departure would not have had the power to destroy him. Criseida's departure, too, is brought about by the course of the war. On a certain day the Trojan forces issue forth as usual under the leadership of Hector to seek battle with the Greeks:

> Vennergli i Greci incontro, e con battaglia
> dura quel giorno consumaron tutto.
>
> [The Greeks came against them and with
> hard battle that day they consumed every-
> thing] (*Filos.* 4.2.1–2).

This abortive sortie and the capture of so many prisoners spell the end for Troilus and Criseida. A prisoner exchange is called for, and when Calchas hears about it, he begins shouting to be noticed (*Filos.* 4.4). He explains again how he came to the Greeks in secret and was the first who brought them hope of success (*Filos.* 4.5). In fact, he claims not only to have promised them victory but also to have shown them how to achieve it (*Filos.* 4.6). He then goes on to claim a favor and asks that they exchange one of their many Trojan prisoners for his daughter, Criseida, whom he was obliged to leave behind when he fled the city in secret. He is successful in his persuasion, and the heroic Antenor is traded for the prophet's daughter (*Filos.* 4.17).[9]

When Criseida leaves Troy, the death of Troilus is brought one step nearer. The final step in his destruction comes when she abandons his love in favor of that of Diomedes. This crucial betrayal, too, is based on the course of the war itself. Diomedes does not persuade Criseida to reject Troilus and take up with him because of his superior charms. He convinces her instead that Troy is doomed, and with Troy, Troilus. When she accepts his view of the war—the view that had motivated her father's escape—she accepts Diomedes as her lover and betrays Troilus.

Diomedes is aware that Troilus and Criseida are lovers (*Filos.* 5.13). He is too stirred up with passion, however, and too well convinced of his own "sovereign artistry" (*Filos.* 6.10.5) to resist at least trying to win her. It is significant that he begins to woo her by sounding out her views on the war:

> E prima seco entrò a ragionare
> dell'aspra guerra tra loro e' Troiani,
> lei domandando quel che le ne pare

[And first he started to speak of the harsh war between them and the Trojans, and asked her what she thought of it] (*Filos.* 6.12.1–3).

When this seemingly casual topic gains some response from her, Diomedes begins to seduce her in earnest. His purpose is to make her transfer her love from Troilus to him; his method is the rather impersonal one of convincing her of the hopelessness of the Trojan position. He tells her that he suspects from her appearance and her manner that she must be in love:

Né so ch'esser si possa la cagione
s'amor non fosse, il qual, se savia sete,
gittrete via, udendo la ragione,
per che, sì com'io dico far dovete:
li Troian son si può dire in prigione
da noi tenuti, sì come vedete,
che siam disposti di non mutar loco,
sanza disfarla con ferro e con foco

[I don't know what could be the reason if love isn't, which, if you are wise, you will get rid of, hearing the reason why, as I say, you should: the Trojans are, you could say, kept in prison by us, as you see, since we are determined not to move from here before destroying [Troy] with iron and fire] (*Filos.* 6.15).

They will punish the crime of Paris (*Filos.* 6.16). Even if there were twelve Hectors, and not one, and even if the prophecies of Calchas were false, they would still be successful (*Filos.* 6.17). He insists, however, that Calchas's prophecies are true:

E non crediate che Calcàs avesse
con tanta istanzia voi raddomandata
se ciò ch'io dico non antivedesse

[And do not imagine that Calchas with such insistence would have asked for you back, if he had

> not foreseen that which I have
> described] (*Filos.* 6.18.1–3).

The point toward which this crescendo of causes has aimed is now made apparent. Diomedes urges:

> Lasciate de' Troian l'amor fallace,
> cacciate via questa speranza amara,
> che 'nvano sospirare ora vi face,
>
> . . . . . .
>
> ch'a tal partito omai Troia è venuta,
> ch'ogni speranza ch'uom v'ha, è perduta
>
> [Give up the false love of the Trojans,
> chase away that bitter hope which now
> makes you sigh in vain . . . for Troy
> is now come to such a pass, that every
> hope men have for her is lost] (*Filos.*
> 6.20.1–4, 7–8).

Criseida replies courteously enough, but she denies her love and asserts her chastity. She does not capitulate to Diomedes immediately, but she lets it be seen that she may soon do so. She reminds him:

> Il tempo è reo, e voi siete nell'armi:
> lascia venir la vittoria ch'aspetti,
> allor saprò io molto me' che farmi:
> forse mi piaceranno più i diletti
> ch'ora non fanno, e potrai riparlarmi
>
> [The time is difficult, and you are
> in arms; let the victory come which
> you await, and then I will know
> better what to do for myself. Per-
> haps then delights will please me
> more than they do now, and you
> may speak with me again] (*Filos.*
> 6.31.1–5).

But Criseida does not wait so long. She is seduced by Diomedes, and the medium he uses is the course of the war and the fated destruction of Troy.[10]

Only one event in Troilus's story remains to be connected with the Trojan setting of the poem, and that is Troilus's death. False hope keeps him alive long after the perfidy of Criseida ought to be apparent. He continues to believe in her until he is forced by a striking circumstance to abandon this faith. Then he seeks and eventually finds his death in battle. Both the precipitating event that spurs his search for death and the death he finds occur in the war.

One day, after a battle between the Greeks and Trojans, Troilus happens to come upon Deiphobos, who has succeeded in taking a rich garment from Diomedes, who has been gravely wounded (*Filos.* 8.8).[11] On this garment is a brooch Troilus had given Criseida. When he sees it, he begins his search for death. There is no doubt that Troilus regards his task as suicidal. He does not anticipate winning the war or even surviving it. He goes instead to find his death. If he can kill Diomedes in the process, this will give him some pleasure (*Filos.* 8.21). Troilus succeeds in destroying many Greeks, although not the one he hates so much, but in the end,

> e dopo lungo stallo,
> avendone già morti più di mille,
> miseramente un dì l'uccise Achille
>
> [and after long delay, having
> killed more than a thousand,
> Achilles killed him one day mis-
> erably] (*Filos.* 8.27.6–8).

So Troilus has the death he longed for and it, too, like all the events of his love affair with Criseida, is found in an episode of the Trojan War.

From this extensive summary, it should be apparent that the love of Troilus and Criseida is linked stage by stage and episode by episode to the events of the war between Greece and Troy. That war does not serve only as a casual background to their love; rather, every aspect of their affair is closely linked with the war itself. Calchas's flight from the Troy he considers doomed implies Criseida's forced separation from Troilus. Before the image of the Palladium, the key to Troy's fall, their love is born. In a bad day of fighting, prisoners are captured whose exchange makes possible the ransoming of Criseida and her removal to the Greek camp. She is seduced by Diomedes when he describes to her the course of the war and the fate of Troy. Troilus is convinced of her perfidy when he sees on Diomedes' cloak, captured in battle, a pin he gave to Criseida. Refusing self-inflicted death, he seeks and finds death in battle. In every episode the private love of the two is linked to the war. Their love, too, is repeatedly checked by reminders of the eventual result of the war. In the flight of Calchas, the image of the Palladium, and the seduction by Diomedes, it is not just the war that is recalled but also its fated outcome. Troy is doomed to destruction by war, just as Troilus is doomed to destruction by love.

In the origin of the war itself there is ample justification for this analogy between the fate of the city and the fate of the lovers. Only one cause is ever stated for the war, and that is Paris's rape of Helen. From the first line of the poem, it is clear that the Greeks have come to Troy to

> vendicar l'oltraggio e la rapina
> da Parìs fatta, d'Elena reina
>
> [avenge that outrage com-
> mitted by Paris, the rape of
> Queen Helen] (*Filos.* 1.7.7–8).

Diomedes describes the Greek purpose in the same terms to Criseida (*Filos.* 6.16). Even Troilus is aware of the injustice of his brother's act and Paris's responsibility for the war (*Filos.* 7.92). All sides are agreed, then, that the fate Troy suffers reflects Paris's rape of Helen. While Paris's motives are not discussed, Troilus does compare his relations with Criseida to those of Paris and Helen and suggests that desire is their common motivation. Pandarus, too, while Criseida is still in Troy, suggests to Troilus that he carry her off, as Paris did Helen. His remarks reinforce the notion that Paris's motivation, like Troilus's, is love or lust (*Filos.* 4.64–65).[12]

While the literary tradition agrees that Paris's rape of Helen precipitated the Trojan War, it is far from unanimous in its judgment of why Troy is destroyed. Homer sees the war as an example of wrath that throws human and even divine law temporarily out of balance. Vergil seems to regard Troy's destruction as the necessary but barely acceptable precondition to Rome's foundation. Dante suggests, in *Inferno* 1, that Troy is destroyed because of pride. Boccaccio is alone when he directly connects Troy's fall with Paris's desire for Helen.[13] He does not make Paris his poem's hero, of course. He uses Troilus to spell out the link between the kind of love that Paris experiences and the death to which it leads. In *Filostrato,* Troilus serves as a step-by-step illustration of how love such as Paris's love for Helen comes to disaster. It also shows the forces in human nature and human society that are brought into play in this destructive process. They are two: moral choice and responsiveness to divine command. The first is the foundation of the poem's allegorical dimension, which Hollander has observed. The second reaches beyond the tropological level to embrace history and divine providence.

That second level of action is given prominence in the poem through a series of implicit and explicit comparisons between the fate of Troilus and the fate of his city, on the one hand, and the fate of those Trojans who escape with Aeneas, on the other. Through these comparisons *Filostrato* suggests that Troilus's moral choices and especially his disobedience to divine command distinguish him from Aeneas and justify the differing fates of those who die in Troy and those who escape to found Rome.

There are several ways in which Troilus is made to resemble Aeneas. In the episode that finally convinces him of Criseida's perfidy, Troilus is characterized in language that engages a famous Vergilian passage. Troilus, seeing the cloak of Diomedes,

> alquanto il tenne;
> e mentre e' rimirava, gli occhi erranti
> or qua or là d'intorno a tutto, avvenne
> che esso vide nel petto un fermaglio
> d'oro, lì posto forse per fibbiaglio.
> Il quale esso conobbe incontanente
>
> [held it awhile and while he was looking, and his eyes were wandering here and there over the whole of it, it happened that he saw on the breast a gold pin put there perhaps as a clasp] (*Filos.* 8.9.4–10.1).

The source of this passage is evidently the famous episode at the end of the *Aeneid,* where the Trojan hero makes a similar discovery. Aeneas is about to bring to an end the war with the Latins and to confirm in the kingdom of Latium the Trojan rights that fate has promised him. His last and greatest opponent lies vanquished at his feet, and Aeneas, in keeping with his father's dictum to "spare the vanquished and beat down the proud" (*Aen.* 6.853), considers mercy for Turnus. While he ponders, his eyes, like Troilus's, wander and light on a significant token (*Aen.* 12.939–44). In Aeneas's case the token is a baldric whose history is as poignant for him as Criseida's pin is for Troilus. This baldric had belonged to Pallas, a young boy whose father, Evander, had placed him under Aeneas's protection. Turnus has killed Pallas and now flaunts his baldric in the face of the man who could not prevent his death. When Aeneas sees and recognizes the spoil Turnus plundered from Pallas's body, "incensed with fury and terrible wrath" (*Aen.* 12.946), he stabs Turnus in the heart. William S. Anderson has argued that "killing Turnus is a victory for the cause, but not for Aeneas. In this final struggle between aspects of *pietas,* Aeneas can only be the loser."[14]

The self-control Aeneas usually achieves eludes him here, and the results are tragic both for his opponent and, in a different way, for himself. Yet his killing of Turnus completes his fated task. When Troilus experiences a madness like that of Aeneas, however, it is merely self-destructive and incapable of preserving Troy.

The love that reaches its tragic peripety here begins in a way that recalls Vergil's treatment of Dido and Aeneas. As Bernhard König has shown, the way Troilus and Criseida fall in love is based on the scene in *Aeneid* 1.441–614, where Dido first encounters the Trojan hero. The love of these two quickly grows to such proportions that Aeneas appears to be abandoning his divinely appointed mission in order to remain in Carthage with the queen. Jupiter sends Mercury (*Aen.* 4.465–76), who urges Aeneas to abandon Carthage and continue his task of founding Rome. Aeneas, despite his disinclination and prompted by a second divine command, eventually agrees. He flees Carthage and heads once again for Italy.

The gods also intervene in Troilus's love life. They send him a dream that reveals Criseida's unfaithfulness. Unlike Aeneas, however, Troilus does not abandon his misplaced love.[15] Even though Troilus's dream is obscure, he immediately realizes its meaning and its divine source. The dream is a harsh one: Troilus

> 'n sogno vide il periglioso
> fallo di quella che 'l facea languire:
> ché gli parea, per entro un bosco ombroso,
> un gran fracasso e spiacevol sentire;
> per che, levato il capo, gli sembiava

un gran cinghiar veder che valicava.
E poi appresso gli parve vedere
sotto a' suoi piè Criseida, alla quale
col grifo il cor traeva, ed al parere
di lui, Criseida di così gran male
non si curava, ma quasi piacere
prendea di ciò che facea l'animale

[saw in a dream the fatal betrayal of her who made him languish: it seemed to him that from within a shady wood he heard a great and distressing sound, and that because of it, he lifted up his head. Then it seemed he saw a great boar breaking out. And then he seemed to see Criseida under its feet, whose heart it pulled out with its tusk; and it seemed to him Criseida didn't mind this great harm, but she almost took pleasure in what the animal did] (*Filos.* 7.23.3–24.6).

Troilus is aware of what the dream means; as he tells Pandarus: "La tua Criseida, oh me, m'ha ingannato" ["Your Criseida, alas, has deceived me"] (*Filos.* 7.26.1). He then explains the dream:

Questo cinghiar ch'io vidi è Diomede.
. . . Oh me, amaro
e vero sogno! Questo l'avrà 'l core
col parlar tratto, cioè 'l suo amore

[This boar I saw is Diomedes . . . Oh me, bitter and true dream. He will have drawn out her heart, that is her love, with his talk] (*Filos.* 7.27.1, 7–8).

His interpretation of the dream is complete, and we, having seen Diomedes at work earlier in the poem, know it to be correct. He believes, moreover, that the dream has been sent to him by the gods: "Gli dii me l'hanno nel sogno mostrato" ["The gods have shown it to me in the dream"] (*Filos.* 7.26.5).

Unlike Aeneas or Calchas, Troilus refuses to act on what he knows to be a true dream sent from the gods. He refuses to change what he calls "his faith" and at Pandarus's suggestion repudiates the dream. Criseida's uncle, who has continually sought to delude him rather than let him be enlightened, begins to contradict the dream and to rebuild Troilus's false hopes. Only the dream makes you mistrust her, he argues (*Filos.* 7.39). Troilus submits and agrees to write to Criseida, as Pandarus suggests, and to confirm the dream in this way, although he has already accused her of skillful deception in words (*Filos.* 7.31). He ends by accepting her ambiguous letter as true and repudiates the divinely sent dream (*Filos.* 7.48). It is only when he sees his brooch on Diomedes' cape that he realizes the dream was indeed true.

> Io veggio pur ch'è vero
> il sogno ed il sospetto e'l mio pensiero
>
> [I see that the dream, my suspicions,
> and my own idea were true] (*Filos.*
> 8.10.7–8).

By then, apparently, it is too late. Whatever good might have come from accepting the truth of the divinely sent dream is now no longer attainable.

It is clear that divine forces do manifest themselves to Troilus as they do to Aeneas. Unlike Aeneas, however, Troilus repudiates what he recognizes as a divinely sent message. It is futile to speculate on what would have happened had he heeded it, but the pattern of Troilus's death search recalls an episode in the *Aeneid* when Aeneas himself, for a little while at least, disregards a divinely inspired dream.

On the night of Troy's destruction, Hector appears to Aeneas in a dream and tells him that the city is doomed and that he must escape (*Aen.* 2.268–97). Aeneas disregards the dream and rushes to the roof of his father's palace to see the battle in progress. Knowing it to be futile and hoping it will be suicidal, he rushes into battle.

> Arma amens capio; nec sat rationis in armis,
> sed glomerare manum bello et concurrere in arcem
> cum sociis ardent animi; furor iraque mentem
> praecipitat, pulchrumque mori succurit in armis
>
> [Frantic, I snatch up arms, there was no use for
> arms, but my spirit burned to mass together a

> group for fighting and to rush to the citadel with my companions; furor and rage drove on my mind: it seemed beautiful to die in arms] (*Aen.* 2.314–17).

Aeneas is maddened with grief and frustration. Throughout the night, dressed in captured Greek armor, he plays out the futile patterns of Iliadic heroism. He will kill, although the war is lost, and he will expose himself to death, since he believes there is no longer anything to live for. Only the intervention of his mother, the goddess Venus, enables him to escape this futile course. She appears to him and asks, "Nate, quis indomitas tantus dolor excitat iras?" ["Son, what pain is so great that it excites this uncontrolled rage?"] (*Aen.* 2.594). Venus then shows her son that Troy's destruction is the work not of men but of the gods. He returns to his home, and when, again with the gods' aid, he wins his father's agreement, he sets off with his family to flee Troy (*Aen.* 2.671–729). No god intervenes to save Troilus, however, and his furious search for death is ultimately successful.

Significantly, long before the composition of Boccaccio's poem, that very death was inscribed in the *Aeneid.* When Aeneas is about to meet Dido, he sees in Carthage on a temple of Juno a series of painted or sculpted scenes. One of these shows Troilus,

> fugiens amissis . . . armis,
> infelix puer atque impar congressus Achilli,
> fertur equis curruque haeret resupinus inani,
> lora tenens tamen; huic cervixque comaeque trahuntur
> per terram, et versa pulvis inscribitur hasta
>
> [the unlucky boy, fleeing disarmed, no match for Achilles, carried away by his horses, still clutching the reins, but entangled; his head and hair dragging the ground and his spear inscribing the dust] (*Aen.* 1.474–78).

In three critical incidents of his life, then, Troilus recalls Aeneas. These reminiscences of Aeneas's career are significant not only because they establish an analogy between the heroes but also because they establish significant differences between the two. Troilus lacks Aeneas's self-control and rejects the divine aid he generally follows. Consequently, his career turns that of Aeneas nearly upside down.

Troilus begins by falling in love with the equivalent of Dido, is maddened by the sight of a jewel such as Pallas's brooch, and seeks and finds death in the Greek assault on Troy. He represents what could have happened to Aeneas had he not continually worked to reestablish control of his emotions and had he failed to heed the counsel of the gods.

Troilus fails to match up to a hero such as Aeneas in part because of his moral failings. That moral nature has historical force as well. By invoking it we might explain why one segment of Troy was doomed and why another survived to found a lasting city. The doomed city possesses the moral character of Troilus (and indeed Paris): it is dominated by lust and wrath, and its uncontrolled emotions lead to its destruction. The remnant that escapes is led by Aeneas, who usually succeeds in controlling his most violent emotions. Self-control is by no means the only force in the careers of Aeneas and of Troilus. While both men make choices on the basis of reason or passion, the gods intervene in the careers of each, and differing responses to divine intervention make important distinctions between the two heroes as well.[16]

Divinity in *Filostrato* is not a casual force reaching down into the lives of men at odd moments. As in the *Aeneid,* discrete divine impulses to action are incorporated into a larger, self-consistent frame of reference that suggests a coherent view of the working of the gods and fate.[17] In *Filostrato,* one passage in particular paints a picture of the cosmos and the place of men and gods within it. When Troilus falls in love with Criseida, he composes a long hymn to Venus (*Filos.* 3.72–89), which springs from and expresses his new affection.[18] This hymn is important in *Filostrato,* for it suggests both the theodicy that governs the poem and Troilus's ultimate understanding of it. In thematic terms, the hymn is divided into two halves, although Troilus makes no formal break in his song. The first section of the poem celebrates an undifferentiated view of love and its tutelary goddess, Venus. Both the earthly and, with equal intensity, the celestial Venus are celebrated. This portion of the hymn ends with the last line of octave 79. At octave 80, Troilus refers more directly to his own situation and cites Hercules as his example and his defense.[19] Although he is not aware of it, the theme of this second portion of the hymn is not only different from but contradictory to the theme of the first half. It celebrates only the earthly Venus.[20] It is finally this lower Venus whom Troilus comes to serve, and the language of the hymn reveals the inadequacy of her deity and the source within it of Troy's disaster.

Troilus's hymn explains that the celestial Venus is responsible for a universal government by desire. This is neither so peculiar nor so ineffectual as it might appear. Aristotelian physics is in part based on the twin forces of "desire" and "hatred," forces that we retain in our own physics under the slightly less emotional terms of "attraction" and "repulsion." It is true, too, as Troilus argues, that procreation is the process that renews the world, that friendship unites families and cities, and that affection softens the will of men and gods. In Troilus's hymn the celestial Venus stands for all the forces and effects of love, friendship, and desire in the animate world and all the processes of governance by attraction in the physical world. As such, she is a fundamental resource of the world below the third heaven, where her planet is found.[21]

Both Troilus and Troy believe themselves to be in perfect consonance with this powerful force, but they are not. They have replaced this celestial Venus with her very different and very inferior earthly aspect. The result is the frustration of all the forces that the higher Venus represents. One has to consider only the fate of Troy and Troilus to see the truth of this. Of the celestial Venus, Troilus observes, "Tu 'l fiero Marte al tuo piacer benegno / ed umil rendi" ["Proud Mars you make humble and compliant to your will"] (*Filos.* 3.77.1–2). But Troy is plagued by war, the work of Mars, and Troilus himself is a primary victim as well as instrument of wrath.

This same contradiction is reiterated when Troilus sings, "Tu dell'amistadi / se' cagion certa e del lor caro frutto" ["You are cause of alliances and of their dear fruit"] (*Filos.* 3.78.3–4). Troy, of course, has no allies, and fights for its life against an invading enemy. Indeed, the fate of Troy is in contradiction to the largest principle of Venus's government:

> Tu legge, o dea, poni all'universo,
> per la quale esso in esser si mantiene
>
> [You give law to the universe goddess by which it maintains itself in being] (*Filos.* 3.79.1–2).

Troy is doomed to extinction, however, precisely because her mode of being is in opposition to that well-regulated one Troilus celebrates. The source of that opposition lies in Troilus's choice of loves and in his refusal to heed the divine impulses that lead him to reject Criseida. Troy's disaster is shadowed by these choices, and the doomed Troy of Troilus and the Troy that reaches safety in Rome with the descendants of Aeneas are distinguished by them.

Filostrato has a historical dimension, then: it is a poem about Troy. It describes that portion of Troy that chose passion in defiance of divinity and perished. Inevitably, it sheds light on that portion of the city that made the opposite choice, and so it describes more than the fate of individual men. The choices of loves and obedience to divinity become social and historical forces. Far from being ornamental, then, the setting of *Filostrato* in Troy reveals the full significance of the poem.

3

Filocolo

Romantic Love and Trojan Remnants

FILOCOLO IS THE LONGEST OF the three texts I examine here. It is the most complex, in terms of both plot and setting, and in many ways the most ambitious. Its unity is often questioned.[1] For these reasons, it has not generally been interpreted as a whole, and the conclusions reached about it have been partial ones. My purpose is to interpret the whole of *Filocolo* and to demonstrate that in significant ways the text's meaning engages the many pagan motifs and episodes within it. I will argue, as I did in the preceding chapter, that the setting of the text in the ancient world and its continual references to the *Aeneid* are not accidental but essential to its meaning.

Filocolo is quite long, and its plot is full of surprises. After an initial allegory based on the *Aeneid* but representing the conquest of the Hohenstaufen rulers of Sicily by the Angevin kings, the fiction itself begins in Rome. There, a young Christian nobleman, Lelio Scipio Africano, descendant of the great Scipios, makes a vow of pilgrimage to Santiago de Compostela if his wife, Giulia Topazia, herself a descendant of the Julian house, is able to conceive. A child is conceived, and Lelio plans to begin his pilgrimage. Giulia Topazia insists on accompanying him, even though the route of pilgrimage passes through territory controlled by the pagan king Felice.

The band of pilgrims, including the pregnant Giulia, soon sets out and at length approaches, somewhere in Spain, the city where Felice is residing. The god Pluto, enraged by the success of the shrine of Saint James in Compostela, plots to destroy this band of Christian pilgrims and to close the borders of Felice's kingdom to further pilgrimage. He disguises himself as a messenger and tells Felice that one of his cities has been destroyed and that a Christian army is now marching directly toward him. This false intelligence is confirmed by the details of a sacrifice to Mars which Felice undertakes. (The details of these two scenes closely reflect the events of *Aeneid* 2 and imitate the false story of Sinon and the gods' apparent confirmation of that story through the death of Laocoön.)

After the Christians have been routed, only Giulia Topazia remains alive. She is brought to Felice's city, where she dies while giving birth to a daughter, Biancifiore. At the same moment, Felice's queen gives birth to a son, Florio. The two fall in love at an early age, but Florio's parents try to prevent their marriage. First, they separate the two; then, hoping to secure Biancifiore's execution, they implicate her in a false plot to murder Felice; when this attempt fails, they sell her to pirates. Florio saves her from execution and eventually finds her in the harem of the admiral of Alexandria. There the lovers are precontracted and consummate their love.

Because Florio violated the seclusion of the harem, the two are condemned to death, a fate from which the gods save them. Now under the protection of the admiral, who turns out to be Florio's maternal uncle, they are married. After their marriage they begin a slow return to Felice's capital, which through most of the text has been Verona, rather than any Spanish city. On the way they visit Rome, where Biancifiore meets her surviving relatives and where Florio, who through the course of his wanderings in search of Biancifiore has assumed the name "Filocolo," is converted to Christianity and returns to his given name. As Christian man and wife, they return to Felice's kingdom. He and all his nation are converted to Christianity, and the territory he controls is once again placed under the suzerainty of Rome and the spiritual leadership of the pope.

This romance is set in the Mediterranean sometime in late antiquity, but it is difficult to fix the date of the story's action. However, two textual references to historical events make it possible to approximate the period of its setting. Early in book 5, Florio and Biancifiore stop near the future site of Certaldo on their return from Alexandria (*Filoc.* 5.38–41). They are told by a band of peasants whom they encounter: "Noi fummo dell'antica città di Fiesole. . . . Ma costoro, non è gran tempo passato, quando Attila guastò la nuova città da' romani fatta a piè della nostra . . . qui fuggirono" ["We were from the ancient city of Fiesole. . . . But these people, not long ago, when Attila destroyed the new city created by the Romans at the foot of ours . . . fled here"] (*Filoc.* 5.39.7–8). Although Boccaccio, in agreement with much medieval tradition, has confused Attila with Totila, the destruction of Florence to which he refers here took place in A.D. 542.[2]

Later in the same book, Ilario, the priest who converts Florio, refers to the emperor Justinian, "il quale alla cattolica fede . . . tornò, non sono ancora molti anni passati, dirizzandolvi Agapito sommo pastore" ["who returned to the Catholic faith . . . not many years ago under the direction of the pope Agapitus"] (*Filoc.* 5.64.5).

Boccaccio's source here is *Paradiso* 6.16–18, where Dante's Justinian records his indebtedness to this pope.[3] Justinian reigned from A.D. 527 to 565. The period of the destruction of Florence and that of Justinian's reign do indeed overlap, and so we ought to imagine that *Filocolo* is set during the reign of Justinian and shortly after the destruction of Florence by Totila—that is, somewhere in the period 542–65.

Once this historical period has been established, it is reasonable to ask whether or not Boccaccio's geographical and historical presentation in *Filocolo* is consistent with it. The answer is necessarily equivocal. Boccaccio does not literally reproduce the historical situation or the geographical distribution of power and worship in this period. In a meaningful sense, however, he represents a central historical problem of the age: the struggles between Romans and non-Romans and between orthodox Christians and their heretical opponents for religious and territorial domination of the Mediterranean world.

Even a summary analysis of details of setting and action reveals the literal inaccuracies and frequent anachronisms in Boccaccio's depiction of the state of affairs in the Mediterranean during the middle of the sixth century. Florio's father, Felice, is often spoken of as "re di Spagna."[4] In Spain Felice inhabits Seville and later Cordova.[5] Most of the action of the text, however, centers in and around a city called Marmorina, which is to be identified with Verona.[6] Felice governs this city and resides in it throughout most of the romance. The true extent of Felice's kingdom is only to be guessed at, but Spain and northern Italy are explicitly included in it. Felice's reign does not appear to include the rest of Italy, however, and near the end of the text, we learn from the priest Ilario that Rome itself is not governed by pagans.[7]

The Goths, like Felice, controlled Spain and Italy in the sixth century.[8] Their kingdom extended the length and breadth of Italy; nevertheless, it is historically accurate to see two competing foci of power in Italy throughout the period of their domination. One, centered in Ravenna, was Gothic and accepted the Arian doctrine subsequently condemned as heretical; the other, centered in Rome, was orthodox and dominated by the old Roman senatorial families. Felice's kingdom, then, reflects the real distribution of influence and orthodoxy, if not the historical boundaries of power. Felice, however, is represented not as an Arian heretic but as a pagan, a worshiper of the old gods, and the most compelling antique recreations within *Filocolo* are devoted to the description of this paganism. Historical Gothic Arianism is represented figuratively here, for reasons I will describe shortly, under the guise of Roman paganism.

History in the text, however, is not confined to this mid-sixth-century setting or to the allegorized portrait of the Christian world divided into orthodox versus "pagan" factions. Felice and his reign are identified both explicitly and metaphorically in a variety of other ways. These identifications contradict the sixth-century setting in historical terms, but they complement it thematically. It is also significant that the events that fix the period when *Filocolo* is set are not referred to until very late in the text. References to Attila and Justinian occur only in the final book. Until that point the exact historical period we are to imagine is left deliberately vague, and the only points of reference are spatial rather than temporal ones. The geography of *Filocolo,* however, suggests familiar and recurrent conditions of the distribution of power and the boundaries of religion in the Mediterranean world throughout Western history.

In *Filocolo,* then, history is pictured not in one moment but in a series of similar and in some sense recurrent moments, each overlaid upon the other. The multiple ethnic and geographical definitions of Felice's kingdom suggest a series of moments in history that cannot coexist in time but that cohere in theme; Felice's kingdom is an abstract historical entity characterized by a recurring antagonism to *Romanitas* and Christianity.

Each identification of Felice and his kingdom is significant of a differing but recurring opposition between historical and religious forces in the Mediterranean. While Felice is the king of Spain, he is also described as the king of Hesperia and successor of Atlas.[9] He is thus the descendant of the leader of the Titans in their struggle against the Olympians.[10] Even as king of Spain, Felice represents more than one thing. Most notably, he serves as a strong counter to both sides of Biancifiore's heritage. Through her father, Lelio Scipio Africano, she is a direct descendant of that Scipio Africanus who first routed the Carthaginians in Spain, then neutralized their campaign in Italy by invading North Africa. He finally overthrew Carthage and destroyed Hannibal in the Second Punic War. His namesake, Scipio Aemilianus Africanus, opposed and destroyed Carthage in the Third Punic War and made Rome the unrivaled power in the Mediterranean. Biancifiore's mother, Giulia Topazia, is, as her name implies, a member of the Julian *gens.* She is thus a descendant of Julius Caesar, who fought a crucial battle against Pompey's forces in Spain in 49 B.C.[11]

When Felice's men are defined as "Arabs," as they are twice in *Filocolo,* yet another historical opponent is suggested.[12] Most obviously, the Arabs are those invaders of Spain who first attacked the Visigothic kingdom in A.D. 711 and quickly established their control over the whole of it. In the eleventh century that control began to be challenged by local rulers, and by the middle of the thirteenth century the *reconquista* was complete in all but name. Cordova in 1236 and Seville in 1248 were among the last cities to be reconquered. After the middle of the thirteenth century, only Granada remained in Moorish hands as a tributary state of Castile.

Felice's Arabs are at one moment described as shooting Parthian arrows.[13] The Parthians were splendid soldiers and bowmen of legendary reputation. They repeatedly made war on Greek and Roman armies. The Christian historian Orosius says they were decisively defeated by Augustus, and at the time of that victory, the gates of the temple of Janus were closed, signifying peace.[14]

The city where Felice resides during most of *Filocolo* is, as I have mentioned, not in Spain but in northern Italy. Called Marmorina in the text, it is to be identified with Verona.[15] Verona does not stand in the text as a representative of Spanish hegemony in Italy; there was none in the sixth or any other century before Boccaccio's death. It represents Gothic hegemony, as I have mentioned, but it also stands as the center within Italy of the control and the intervention there of the Holy Roman emperors. Verona and the Veronese territories were long preserved by these German rulers as their gateway into Italy. Hence, Verona represents the antagonistic imperial presence in Italy. First checked in the mid-thirteenth century by the sudden death of Frederick II, it was finally overcome by the Angevin victories over Manfred in 1265 and the execution of Conradin in 1268. These events are alluded to in the initial allegory of *Filocolo.* In a metaphorical way, although not explicitly, Felice is identified with the Trojan king Priam.[16] In *Filocolo* 1, Felice takes part in a series of episodes based on *Aeneid* II, in which he plays a role analogous to that of the great Trojan king.

The Olympian victory over the Titans and Manfred's defeat are thus the temporal boundaries within which the history embraced by Felice's multiple identities is played out. Within this great space of time, particular events are especially called to mind. If one adds other events alluded to in the text, such as Justinian's conquest of Italy, mentioned by Ilario, and Charlemagne's conquest of the Lombards, alluded to in *Filocolo* 1.1.5, the list becomes substantial. I will later emphasize the central event of *Filocolo* 1.3.5, Christ's "conquest" of the pagan gods, as the most significant event in the text; I include it here in anticipation. The events are as follows:

1. The conquest by the Olympian gods of the Titans
2. The destruction by the Olympian gods of Troy
3. The conquest by Scipio of Carthage
4. The conquest by Julius Caesar of rebellious Spain
5. The conquest by Augustus of Parthia
6. The conquest by Christ of the pagan gods
7. The reconquest by Justinian of Italy
8. The conquest by Charlemagne of the Lombards
9. The *reconquista* by Christians of Spain
10. The defeat by the Angevins of the Hohenstaufen

It is not clear that ten such events and only ten are alluded to in *Filocolo*. Their number is not necessarily significant; what clearly is of significance, however, is their historical thrust. The original event in this series, the triumph of the Olympian gods over their Titanic opponents, sets out in metaphorical form the issue that Boccaccio feels underlies each of the other struggles. In every case, one warring faction fights either for the establishment of the Roman Empire or for the establishment or reestablishment of Christian ascendancy over a pagan enemy.

Vergil is the most significant of the many Augustan writers who conceived of the foundation of the Roman Empire not as a secular but as a divinely appointed task. The historical vision of the *Aeneid* forms a primary link, then, between the struggle of the Olympians and Titans and the Carthaginian wars or the battles of the Roman civil war. Vergil presents these historical battles as earthly manifestations of the divine struggle to create Rome and to unify it under Augustus. So, in the most general terms, Felice's kingdom represents the historical enemies of Rome aided by misguided deities (analogous to the Titans) in their futile opposition to Jupiter and the

Fates. Biancifiore's ancestry represents those families, the Scipiones and the Julii, who with divine aid overcame such opponents.

In Boccaccio's text, however, Vergil's historiography is given a Christian and providential thrust, and for this transformation of his primary source Boccaccio is indebted to Paulus Orosius. Orosius argues that the purpose of founding the Roman Empire was satisfied not by the reign of Augustus in itself but only by the Incarnation of Christ, which occurred during that reign.[17] In general, it is Orosius's purpose to show "ut per omnia venturi Christi gratia praeparatum Caesaris imperium conprobetur" ["that it is proved by all things that the grace of the Christ to come was prepared by the *imperium* of Caesar"].[18]

The empire of Augustus is thus, in Orosius's view, the divinely appointed last event, but not the goal, of Roman history. Accordingly, events such as the subjection by Scipio of Hannibal or the destruction of Carthage by his descendant are now to be linked in a providential chain culminating in the Incarnation.[19] The struggle to found the Roman Empire is a divine task carried out for a purpose that ultimately exceeds the intentions of the Roman gods. Orosius sees it within the framework of the Christian God's general governance of the world.[20] In his view Roman history is only one part of the larger providential scheme by which the whole world has always been governed, even though men have been largely ignorant of the true God.

Boccaccio knew Orosius's *Histories* well and was interested enough in its contents to copy substantial portions of it in one of his notebooks, known as the *Zibaldone Magliabechiano.*[21] The parts that interested him particularly were the last two books, which cover the period from the fall of the republic to the reign of Emperor Honorius. These he copied extensively and supplemented with material from other Latin and early Christian historians.[22] Boccaccio continues Orosius's history by adding to it Martinus Polonus's *Chronicle of Popes and Emperors,* which brings Orosius's providential story down to the reign of Frederick II.

Just as they do in Boccaccio's *Zibaldone Magliabechiano,* Orosius's work and his point of view about the providential nature of Roman history underlie the fiction of *Filocolo;* and the providential pattern that Orosius sees is carried on in that romance through reference to events in the Christian period. Four later historical events, as I have already observed, are recalled by the various identifications of Felice, his kingdom, and his men. These include the mid-sixth-century reconquest of Italy by Justinian, alluded to in the final book of *Filocolo;* Charlemagne's conquest of the Lombards; the expulsion of the Arab invaders of Spain in the *reconquista;* and the Hohenstaufen presence in Sicily that is finally overcome by Charles of Anjou.

In the introduction to *Filocolo,* Boccaccio presents a historical situation in allegorical terms, and this passage serves as an example of how to read *Filocolo.* This unexpected and complex allegory presents itself in terms of the *Aeneid.* It recounts the continuing wrath of Juno against a last remnant of the Trojans. The traditional motives for Juno's anger at the Trojans, as Vergil records them, are recalled, and Aeneas's desertion of Dido ranks high among them. Juno here accuses Aeneas not only of desertion but also of the violation of a marriage contract.[23] Juno's second complaint centers on the judgment of Paris. In *Filostrato,* as I have described, Paris chooses lust and the earthly Venus. Like Troilus's city, the "Trojan remnant" of this allegory (*Filoc.* 1.1.7–11) is also characterized as lustful. Juno's grudges against the Trojans, then, are the traditional ones. What is most surprising in *Filocolo* is the historical identity of the group to whom the name "Trojans" is applied.

We soon learn that Juno's minister on earth is the pope, who "held the holy office through her" ("per lei tenea il santo ufficio"), and that the remnant of the Trojans is not, as we are accustomed to think, the faction whose leader is Aeneas, the man outstanding for goodness, but the very opposite. For once in the tradition of the *Aeneid,* our sympathies are understood to be with Juno and against "Aeneas."[24] More precisely, we are expected to be against the remnant of Aeneas's "faction." (As we will soon see, however, that means being for, not against, the historical Aeneas.) Juno's purpose in coming to her chief priest, the pope, is to urge him to enlist the aid of a "valoroso giovane" descended from Charlemagne, that is, Charles of Anjou, as champion against the "Trojans." The pope is eager to obey, and Juno promises him supernatural aid. She declares her intention to visit again the kingdom of Pluto and enlist, as she did before, Allecto's help against the Trojans.[25]

In recalling her earlier harrassment of the Trojans, she clarifies her opposition to their offshoot and confirms the providential view of history advanced by Orosius. She depicts herself, in contradiction to Vergil, not as having failed to destroy the Trojans but as having refused to do so. Her reasons were two: she wished to give the Trojans time to "repent" and "earn pardon," and she knew that from them would descend Romulus, the founder, as she calls him, of "this pontifical place." These two reasons are closely linked; indeed, they are really two ways of suggesting the same event, that is, the moment when the city of Rome becomes the pontifical city and when, at the same moment, the Romans themselves, descendants of the Trojans, become Christians. Juno describes herself as sparing these Trojans who would eventually "repent" and "earn pardon" by becoming Christians.

Our sympathies and the sympathies of Juno are therefore not directed against these Trojans who became first Romans and then Christians. They are directed, instead, at an imagined group of Trojans who either resisted this process of conversion or returned to an earlier Trojan identity. There is no clear precedent for such a fiction in the *Aeneid.*[26] No renegade band refuses to give up its Trojan identity and become Roman when the war in Italy is concluded. Nevertheless, conversion from a Trojan to a Roman fate and a parallel conversion from a Trojan to a Roman identity are strong themes in the *Aeneid.*[27] As Boccaccio shows in *Filostrato,* too, there are two sides to the Trojan personality: the libidinous and impious aspects, which are punished by the destruction of Troy, and the pious and self-controlled aspects, which are rewarded with Aeneas.

Boccaccio presents the enemies of Juno as men who have attempted to bring back to life a Troy that has not passed through this process of historical conversion. He presents them in imagery that suggests a kind of unnatural growth. They are "a little branch . . . that schemed to reinvigorate the already dead roots at their trunk" (*Filoc.* 1.1.1). More particularly, they are "the false shoots" above the withered branches and the dry roots (*Filoc.* 1.1.1). Such offshoots do not represent the true growth of the tree, which has long passed into history. They are, instead, parasitic upon their great parent. This imagery of unnatural growth in Juno's enemies is opposed on the side of her allies by true fruitfulness and generative power. Against the unnatural offshoots whose characteristic crimes are libidinous, Charles of Anjou is finally successful.[28]

Such a dialectic is characteristic of sermons of the Crusades and of polemics against pagans and heretics in general. In fact, the primary model for the portrayal of the Hohenstaufen as anachronistic

"Trojans" is not Vergilian but biblical. Its roots lie in a Christian spiritualizing of Old Testament language. By its application, the Israelites who received God's covenant are divided into two groups: one is the historical but unconverted Israel, the other, the spiritual but ahistorical one. Paul carefully distinguishes these two groups: "For they are not all Israelites who are sprung from Israel; nor because they are the descendants of Abraham, are they all his children; but 'Through Isaac shall thy posterity bear thy name.' That is to say, they are not sons of God who are the children of the flesh, but it is the children of promise who are reckoned as posterity."[29]

Boccaccio appears to have translated such a distinction between physical and spiritual descendants into Vergilian terms. The Troy that followed its fate and changed its identity to Roman, as Vergil describes, and to Roman Christian, in Boccaccio's allegory, is like the Israel that is called "the children of promise." The false shoots that the dead trunk of Trojan history throws off are, like "the children of the flesh," an outmoded remnant of the past.

What Boccaccio does in this introductory allegory prepares the reader to understand the complex role history plays in *Filocolo.* As I have noted, several elements combine in that allegory to give it shape. In its recollection of Juno and the Trojans, it casts itself in Vergilian form.[30] The prologue's reading of the *Aeneid,* moreover, accentuates Vergil's own insistence on the divinely sponsored destiny of Rome.[31] Boccaccio, following Vergil, sees the Trojans as Romulus's forebears and hence as founders of Rome.[32] He goes one step further than Vergil, however, and follows Orosius when he extends the Trojan heritage into the Christian period. By seeing Aeneas and his band as founders of Christian Rome, he is asserting not only the intervention and the interest of divinity but also the interest of Providence in the Trojans' fate. This providential turning prepares for the final element of the allegory: Boccaccio, apparently following a biblical model, imagines the Hohenstaufen and their antipapal followers as false "Trojans," that is, false Christians. They bear the same relation to true Trojans that the Israel of the flesh bears to the Israel of the promise. These false Trojans are a historical anachronism and a spiritual one. They should be converted as the true Trojans and the true Israel were. Instead, like the Israel of the flesh, they assume an old identity, the validity of which has long been superseded.

This introductory allegory is integrated with Felice's multiple identifications. On such a basis the whole historical framework of *Filocolo* is built. Each of the kingdoms identified with Felice's realm has been an opponent of Rome or of Roman Christianity. What is most curious and revealing about this list is that it comprises only defeated enemies. No historical opponent of Rome or of Christianity that was not defeated in the past is alluded to. The Titans have long been defeated by the Olympians. The threat of Carthage is overcome by Scipio Africanus. The Spanish followers of Pompey in the first century B.C. were overcome by Julius Caesar, and Augustus, his heir, defeated the Parthians. Justinian conquered the Goths, and Charlemagne, the Lombards. The Arabs in Spain have finally been brought under control by the *reconquista* of the mid-thirteenth century. Verona represents the defeated Hohenstaufen. Felice's own kingdom, however, while it recalls a series of defeated enemies, remains an antagonist to Rome and to Christianity for most of the text. In effect, it is as if the defeated enemies metaphorically implied by that kingdom had not been conquered at all. What is represented metaphorically, moreover, is also represented in another way.

As I have noted, Felice's religion and that of his son are painstakingly presented in pagan terms. This curious feature represents a historical anachronism, of course; Felice and his subjects should be Arian Christians. However, Felice's religion is not so much a historical portrayal as a reflection in a different mode of the conquered-enemy theme. Felice is a Roman pagan, while the Rome he opposes is already Christian. His paganism, then, like the metaphorical opponents he recalls, shows him as the conquered enemy mysteriously resuscitated. He is atavistic Roman paganism brought to life in the same way that the "Trojan" remnant was brought to life in the imagery of the initial allegory.

Historical Roman religion as Felice practices it thus serves a significant thematic role in the text. It is not by any means a simple anachronism. It represents Boccaccio's Romanization of the imagery of heresy and of the individual's falling away from faith in Christ to something essentially pre-Christian.[33] The central theme of the text centers on Felice's antagonism to Rome and Rome's response to that antagonism. In essence, that conflict is carried out in two quite opposite ways. Felice, at satanic instigation, slaughters Christian pilgrims whom he perceives as aggressors in his kingdom. The

Christian pilgrims, with explicit divine sanction, respond in kind (*Filoc.* 1.25.9–10). Their principal form of aggression, however, is the ironic gift they leave behind in Felice's kingdom: Biancifiore.

In *Filocolo* 1.1.12, Felice performs a complex sacrificial rite that plainly recalls the Laocoön scene in *Aeneid* 2, and the scene immediately preceding recalls the deception of Sinon. The imitation of these episodes from the *Aeneid* plays a part in an even more extensive adaptation of that text in *Filocolo.* In the *Aeneid,* the purpose of both Sinon's deceit and the gods' destruction of Laocoön is the same: to make the Trojans accept the horse.[34] In *Filocolo* a similar purpose is served. Felice marches against a small Christian force and destroys it. Thus, like the Trojans, he believes his enemy has disappeared, and, also like the Trojans, he takes in something belonging to the enemy. It is the apparently innocent Giulia Topazia, but she, like the Trojan horse, has something hidden inside her.[35] That something, Biancifiore, will eventually prove as successful in overrunning Felice's kingdom as the Greeks proved in overrunning Priam's Troy. She does not destroy the kingdom by killing Felice or his men, as the Greeks destroyed Troy; she subverts Felice's reign by bringing about its conversion (in fact, reconversion) to Christianity. Through Biancifiore's love for Florio and his love for her the conversion of Felice's kingdom from atavistic paganism to the true Roman religion is brought about.

The love story of Florio and Biancifiore intersects the providential allegory that Felice's kingdom suggests. Like the story of Troilus, it shows the forces in the individual life that both respond to and provoke the providential shaping of history. Three factors are involved: love, response to divine suggestion, and virtuous action. Two of these factors shape the story of Troilus, as we have seen, and they operate in analogous fashion in *Filocolo.* The difference between the two stories, and the force that separates the fate of Florio and Biancifiore from the fate of Troilus, is the differing nature of their loves and of their responses to divinity. Troilus deprives his love of its celestial nature. Florio and Biancifiore experience intense passion, but their love never loses its attachment to the divine. Troilus, as we know, ignores the promptings of the gods, but Florio and Biancifiore continually collaborate with the divinities who aid them. This obedience to divine command, moreover, enables Florio to use his skill as a warrior in the service of virtue and not, as Troilus does, in pursuit of self-destruction. Through their love, their obedience to divine suggestion, and their virtuous action, Florio and Biancifiore earn their place in a Troy that, in Boccaccio's view, becomes not only Roman but Christian. Troilus, who made the opposite choices, belongs, as I have shown, to the doomed and carnal Troy that Felice's kingdom symbolizes. Through the power of their love, Florio and Biancifiore subvert this kingdom and bring about its ultimate conversion to *Romanitas* and Christianity. In the first part of this fable, the pagan gods are responsible for carrying out what eventually becomes an explicitly Christian providential scheme, and the Venus Urania whom Troilus rejects is the divinity most active in the early adventures of Florio and Biancifiore.

After the death of Giulia Topazia, Biancifiore is taken in by Felice and his queen and raised with their newborn son, Florio. The children dress alike and play together; they are placed under the same master for instruction. It is only at this point that the danger Biancifiore represents begins to become manifest. The instruction the two children receive is directed precisely toward the awakening of Biancifiore's conquering power, love. The children, under their master, Racheio, begin to study the works of the pagan authority in that discipline: "E loro in brieve termine insegnate conoscer le lettere, fece loro leggere il santo libro d'Ovidio, nel quale il sommo poeta mostra come i santi fuochi di Venere si deano ne' freddi cuori con sollecitudine accendere" ["And having taught them in a brief time to know their letters, he had them read the holy book of Ovid, in which the great poet shows how with care the holy fires of Venus are to be lit in cold hearts"] (*Filoc.* 1.45.6).

As Quaglio recognizes, the allusion is to the *Ars amatoria*, a common introductory schoolbook throughout the Middle Ages.[36] This discipline soon produces its anticipated result, and the fires of Venus, the mistress, in any case, of the children's ascendant, are kindled in the hearts of Florio and Biancifiore.[37] This is both a good thing and a bad thing.[38] To the extent that a physical passion is aroused in two inexperienced children, it brings the usual dangers. But theirs is not simply a private passion. Venus soon takes a hand in it in a way that once again recalls the framework of the *Aeneid* and the providential scheme to which that text is linked.

The second book of *Filocolo* begins with Venus's journey to Citherea to visit her son, Cupid, whom she finds "temperante nuove saette nelle sante acque" ["tempering new arrows in the holy waters"] (*Filoc.* 2.1.2). The combination of "tempering," "new," and "holy" in this brief passage suggests an unfamiliar Cupid, linked to a moderate, new, and holy love. Nevertheless, this love will serve a militant purpose, and Venus's request to her son has a decidedly familiar ring. She describes the place where Florio and Biancifiore are, and tells how they "invocano con casti cuori il nostro nome, disiderando d'essere del numero de' nostri suggetti" ["invoke our name with chaste hearts, desiring to be in the number of our subjects"] (*Filoc.* 2.1.3). Then she instructs him in the best way to inspire them with love: "E come già nella non compiuta Cartagine prendesti forma del giovane Ascanio, così ora ti vesti del senile aspetto del vecchio re, padre di Florio; e quando se' là ove essi sono, sì come egli quando va a loro gli abbraccia e bacia costretto da pura benivolenza, così tu, abbracciandoli e baciandoli, metti in loro il tuo segreto fuoco, e infiamma sì l'un dell'altro, che mai il tuo nome de' loro cuori per alcuno accidente non se ne spenga" ["And as you once when Carthage was not yet finished took the form of the young Ascanius, so this time dress yourself in the face of the old king, the father of Florio, as he is when he goes to them, embraces them and kisses them, constrained by pure goodwill; so you, embracing and kissing them, put in them your secret fire, and so inflame them one with another that your name by no occurrence may ever be extinguished from their hearts"] (*Filoc.* 2.1.5).

The reference to Carthage and to Ascanius is extremely significant, for by it Venus identifies the aim of this enamorment with the earlier one. In *Aeneid* 1, she tells Cupid of her fears and her motives for wishing to dominate Dido through love for Aeneas: "You know that your brother Aeneas is tossed on the sea and upon every shore by the hatred of bitter Juno, and you have often grieved with our grief. Now Phoenician Dido holds and delays him with flattering words, and I deeply mistrust where this Junonian hospitality might lead."[39]

This extraordinary passage shows Venus plotting to bring about the fated arrival of Aeneas in Rome and scheming to anticipate whatever her rival might intend to try on her home ground. Reference to it in *Filocolo* is in no sense incidental. Venus is once again using Cupid here, as in the *Aeneid*, to overthrow a kingdom hostile to the mission of her people.[40]

Venus's plot is carried out, and she protects the young lovers in later episodes.[41] When Felice is told by Racheio and Ascalion that Florio and Biancifiore are in love, his opposition to that love begins and with it the need for Venus's protection (*Filoc.* 2.6.2). Felice sees this new love as a threat to everything he possesses. Fortune, Felice argues, will undo his triumphs by depriving him of his son (*Filoc.* 2.7.6–8). He sees the love between the children and sees Biancifiore herself as a threat to his enjoyment of his kingdom. He feels she will pose an even more direct threat in the future: "Non è questa gran cagione di dolersi pensando che un sì fatto giovane, il quale ancora dee sotto il suo imperio governare questi regni, sia per una feminella perduto?" ["Is this not great cause for unhappiness, that a youngster like this, who must govern these kingdoms under his rulership, should be lost for the sake of an inconsequential girl?"] (*Filoc.* 2.7.10).[42]

This complaint is answered by the queen, who suggests that the children simply be kept apart (*Filoc.* 1.8.3). This plan, however, is futile, as an authorial aside informs us: "Ma, oh quanto fu tale imaginazione vana, con ciò sia cosa che durissimo sia resistere alle forze de' superiori corpi, avvenga che possibile!" ["But oh how vain that plan was, inasmuch as it is extremely difficult to resist the forces of the heavenly bodies, if that is even possible!"] (*Filoc.* 2.9.2).[43]

Indeed, the queen's perfectly reasonable plan does not succeed, and Felice becomes aware that Florio is getting worse, not better. The queen, "inflamed with wrath" at this news, responds: "Or chi dubita che mentre che Biancifiore viverà, Florio mai non la dimenticherà? Certo no, e questo è manifesto" ["Now who doubts that while Biancifiore is alive, Florio will never forget her? Certainly not, and this is obvious"] (*Filoc.* 2.38.3, 2.28.3).

The queen begins to hatch a plot against Biancifiore that will give their desire to murder her some color (*Filoc.* 2.28). The king, while he confesses his past and continuing affection for her, foresees less damage from her death than from her life, and he tells his seneschal of the plot he has concocted against her (*Filoc.* 2.29.4–12). They act quickly and, in the course of a great dinner, have her bring in a poisoned peacock to the king.[44] Biancifiore's apparent intent to murder the king is exposed when a dog eats a morsel of the bird and dies. The seneschal declares that Biancifiore should be burned at the stake, and the king agrees (*Filoc.* 2.76.2). Judges, however, cannot pass sentence on this holiday, so Biancifiore is arrested, but not, as the king wishes, suddenly put to death (*Filoc.* 2.39.4, 2.40.1).

It is at this point that Venus intervenes to save Biancifiore. She sends Florio a dream in which he sees a disruption of the earth and the heavens so extraordinary and violent that it makes him wonder: "Intende Giove di fare l'universo tornare in caos come già fu?" ["Does Jove intend to return the world to chaos as it once was?"] (*Filoc.* 2.42.6). He sees the gods themselves in great sorrow: "Gli parve vedere i regni di Giove pieni di sconforto, e gl'iddii piangendo visitare le sedie l'uno dell'altro" ["He seemed to see the kingdom of Jove full of discomfort, and the gods weeping and visiting each other's thrones"] (*Filoc.* 2.42.3).

This dream clearly portends disaster, and its form reveals the extreme importance Biancifiore has in the eyes of all the gods. Venus here, as in the *Aeneid,* is the chief instrument by which the divine will is brought to bear in human affairs, and she now appears to Florio and asks him: "Oimè, misera . . . or etti occulta la cagione del pianto degli uomini, dell'aere e degl'iddi? Levati su, che io la ti mostrerò" ["Oh miserable me . . . is the cause of the weeping of men, the winds, and the gods hidden from you? Get up, so that I can show it to you"] (*Filoc.* 2.42.7).

She then shows him the whole plot against Biancifiore. Florio asks, "Tu mi mostra qual via c'è alla difensione della sua vita" ["Show me what way there is for the defence of her life"] (*Filoc.* 2.42.10).

Venus assures him that Biancifiore's life can and indeed will be saved; the gods have foreseen this and decided it already (*Filoc.* 2.92.11). Nevertheless, she is eager to achieve it not through her own activity but through the work of Florio. This, of course, is the very principle of providential history. The gods foresee, they plan and scheme, but they are allied with men, if not to some degree even dependent on human action to bring these plans to fruition. Because men do the gods' will, history becomes providential. When they refuse their suggestion, as Troilus does, they and their cities suffer disaster. Venus thus tells Florio exactly what he is to do to rescue Biancifiore and promises him the aid of many gods (*Filoc.* 2.42.16–19).

The goddess of love has obtained the aid of the chaste moon, whose "cold light" will guide Florio. Not only Mars, her "dearest love," but also her "husband," Vulcan, will lend his aid. Thus the portrait of divine intervention that emerges is not only one of a collaborative effort but one of an unusual reconciliation among gods of opposite natures. The importance of Florio's undertaking is underscored in this way, and it is reaffirmed by the sword Venus gives him, which was created especially for the gods' battle against the

Titans.[45] This sword helps to identify the battle against Felice with that exemplary struggle.

Providence, in the person of this active divinity, has seen to all these preparations. Florio awakens with the Titan-killing sword in his hand. During the same night, Venus hastens to appear in the cell of Biancifiore, and not in a dream but in person: "Nella prigione subitamente apparve una gran luce e maravigliosa, dentro alla quale Venere ignuda, fuor solamente involta in uno porporino velo, coronata d'alloro, con un ramo delle frondi di Pallade in mano dimorava" ["In the prison suddenly appeared a great and marvelous light, within which Venus stood nude, except that she was wrapped in a purple veil, crowned with laurel and with a branch of the leaves of Pallas in her hand"] (*Filoc.* 2.48.16).

This unusual Venus reconciles in her eclectic attributes the same opposites that her allies represent in Florio's dream. Here she is nude—the way she best displays her particular weapons—yet armed with the lance of Apollo and bearing the olive of Minerva.[46] These are gods of reason and wisdom. As Florio's dream suggests a kind of chaste but impassioned militancy, Venus here suggests a fusion of wisdom and reason with her own sensuality. The fusion of these apparent contradictions is suggested in yet another way: Venus's apparition in a prison and her consolatory purpose recall Philosophia, who appears to Boethius in similar circumstances.[47] As her more decorously dressed exemplar has done, Venus consoles the prisoner awaiting execution. She tells Biancifiore, as Lady Philosophy cannot tell Boethius, that "da questa ora avanti niuna cosa ti sarà fatta, per la quale altra offesa che sola un poco di paura te ne seguisca" ["from this hour on nothing will be done to you from which any harm other than a little fear will follow"] (*Filoc.* 2.48.18).

She explains to Biancifiore, too, as Philosophia reveals to her follower, that her allegiance is the cause of her present danger: "Niuna altra cagione ci è, se non per che tu e Florio siete al mio servigio disposti" ["There is no other cause than that you and Florio are devoted to my service"] (*Filoc.* 2.48.22).[48]

Despite the god's vigilance, Biancifiore's life is still threatened. It is human weakness, however, not divine inattention, that nearly causes Biancifiore's death. During the night, Florio and Ascalion have reached a place near where Biancifiore is to be executed. Because of the lateness of the hour, their excitement, and their fatigue, they fall asleep (*Filoc.* 2.55). Boccaccio, in an authorial intrusion that gives the impression of trying to awaken these characters, reminds them that "Venus ha infino a qui fatto il suo dovere: se tu a quello ch'ella t'ha detto sarai pigro, ella si riderà di te, e terratti vile, e scherniratti con dovute beffe" ["Venus has up to now done her duty: if you are slothful in the face of what she has told you, she will laugh at you, and consider you a coward, and scorn you with well-deserved mockery"] (*Filoc.* 2.56.4).

Not only is Florio asleep, however: he dreams of having saved Biancifiore and believes he is already kissing her in a pleasant garden: "Allora l'altissimo prencipe delle battaglie, sollecitato dalla sua amica, discese del suo cielo, e sopra un rosso cavallo, armato quanto alcun cavaliere fosse mai, sopragiunse a costoro" ["And then the highest prince of battles, begged by his lover, descended from his sphere, and riding a red horse, more heavily armed than any horseman had ever been, he arrived where Florio was"] (*Filoc.* 2.57.4).

Mars awakens the slothful Florio and Ascalion, and together they go into battle against the oppressors of Biancifiore. This episode underscores once more the importance of human participation in the divinely appointed task and the way a vice like slothfulness can interfere with the human response to divine suggestion. Once in battle, Florio is brave and effective. He kills the wicked seneschal, who confesses the plot against Biancifiore, although he does not reveal the king's role in it, and clears Biancifiore's name. Biancifiore is restored, at least outwardly, to her former position in the court. On their return home, Ascalion and Felice dedicate their arms to Mars, and Florio receives from Venus the victor's crown, which he immediately rededicates to her (*Filoc.* 2.75).

This is not the end of Venus's aid to the lovers. She is still active in their behalf late in book 4, when she prevents the admiral's blade from killing Florio and Biancifiore (*Filoc.* 4.126). Then she obtains the consent of all the gods to save the lives of the two.[49] In this crucial episode, moreover, she announces to them, "Questa sarà ultima ingiuria a voi e fine delle vostre avversità, dopo la quale voi pacificamente, avendo vinta la contraria fortuna, viverete. Io v'ho recato segnale di pace. . . . E questo detto, lasciato l'ulivo nelle loro mani si partì" ["This will be the final injury to you and the end of your adversity, after which you will live having conquered your contrary fortune. I have brought you the sign of eternal peace. . . . And having said this, and having left the olive in their hands, she departed"] (*Filoc.* 4.134.3–4).

It is true, as the goddess predicts, that from this time on cease the disasters that have plagued Florio and Biancifiore since the moment their love was discovered. They are liberated from this final trial by the *ammiraglio* of Alexandria, and when Florio reveals his name and kinship, it quickly becomes clear that, far from being his enemy, the admiral is his mother's brother. With great pomp and expense the lovers are married publicly in Alexandria.[50] After much delay they set out in the direction of Rome.

In short, then, Venus and, at her instigation, the other gods (principally Jove and Mars) continually support and preserve Florio and Biancifiore. And in this sense the providential history alluded to in various ways in the introductory allegory is echoed in its main plot. Venus's continual solicitude is the means by which the larger plan that the gods have in mind for Florio and especially for Biancifiore is carried out.[51] Constantly required, however, is the virtue and goodwill of the lovers. Without the disposition to do the divine will and the strength of purpose to pursue it, the heavenly intention would fail. The gods wish Florio and Biancifiore to marry. When this end, which indirectly recalls Juno's presence in the introductory allegory, is achieved for them, adversity is ended, and the gods retire victorious.[52] However, their marriage, which is precisely the event that Felice has worked so determinedly and with so little success to present, is not the end of *Filocolo.* An entire book remains in which first Florio and Biancifiore and then Felice and his entire kingdom are converted to Christianity. This conversion occurs only because Biancifiore wishes to visit the city of her parents, and there, seemingly by chance, Florio is converted. It is finally when he receives Christian baptism that Florio, who has long used the name Filocolo, returns to his given name, and it is only at this moment that the providential purpose seems to have finally been satisfied.[53]

This love story is Boccaccio's vehicle for linking providential history with the life of individuals.[54] It takes Florio and Biancifiore from the time of her conception to the moment when, as Christian man and wife and as the children of Christians and Christian converts, they finally assume control over Felice's kingdom, returned at last to the suzerainty of Rome. Their response to the divine presence in their lives echoes the divine role in the history of which they are part.

The love of Florio and Biancifiore brings about all of the significant results in the text. Scipio, however, does not conquer Africa through love, nor does Charles of Anjou overcome Manfred through love. Wrath is the means in these cases. Boccaccio, however, has imagined a fiction that stands against these historical conquests, and by its terms the medium of conquest, or of reconquest, is not wrath but love. Biancifiore represents love's power to bring about the conversion of Florio, Felice, and all their kingdom. Considering Biancifiore, then, in terms of her initial presentation in the allegory of the first book of *Filocolo,* it is evident that this innocent child in the Trojan horse of her mother's womb poses no threat of violence to Felice's kingdom. Yet she does threaten him, and he reacts with increasing but unavailing rigor. Finally, like the Greek soldiers who sprung from the horse's belly and burned Troy, she succeeds in overthrowing Felice's kingdom. She does so by winning the love of Florio and, through this love, winning his kingdom for baptism and for the eternal Rome that is both the church and, as in Dante's view, paradise itself.

It is the greatest mystery of *Filocolo* that this process is begun and furthered by the pagan gods. How is it that these deities are so eager to aid and protect Biancifiore, and yet, when Florio and Biancifiore are freed from the fire and married, these gods are not given a further thought? Florio, the man who has enjoyed their favor and company throughout his troubled life, nevertheless receives baptism, "confessando la santa credenza e rinunziando la iniqua" ["confessing the holy faith and renouncing that wicked one"] (*Filoc.* 5.71.17). That "wicked" faith he had proclaimed at his first meeting with the priest who converts him: "Da noi è adorato Giove, e gli altri immortali iddii posseditori delle celestiali regioni a' quali, quante volte di loro abbiamo bisogno, tante volte acendiamo fuochi sopra i loro altari e diamo incensi, e le dimandate cose riceviamo" ["Jove is worshiped by us and the other immortal gods, possessors of the heavenly regions, to whom, as often as we have need of them, we light fires above their altars and give incense; and we receive the things we ask"] (*Filoc.* 5.52.7).

After his conversion, Florio renounces the very gods whose faith he earnestly confesses and whose effectiveness he has proved. This is never explicitly discussed by Boccaccio, but it need not be. The reason is explained by history, at least as Orosius views it. It is God himself who has operated through the pagan divinities here, just as in Orosius's scheme of things he operates in the *Aeneid* throughout Roman history. At the moment of conversion the veil disguising this fact is destroyed, and Christianity and the Christian God naturally replace the ambiguous names under which they were figured.[55] The pagan gods disappear from *Filocolo* precisely as they disappeared from history. The conversion of Florio, like the conversion of history at the moment of the Incarnation, is the moment when their influence ceases to be felt.

In the heart of the individual, the pagan gods represent the forces for both good and evil, for both order and chaos, with which every man must struggle. At the moment of conversion these forces are brought into a new order under the government of God and the Holy Spirit. The work of conversion is never complete, however. Each new man is born with his old gods intact, and each must struggle to achieve their conquest by Christianity. In history we see this as a pattern of falling away from Christianity. We see the conquered territories lapsing again into paganism—as Spain did, as Sicily did under the Hohenstaufen, as Felice's kingdom did. *Filocolo* shows by what means those kingdoms that have fallen away are won again. Into each heart God sends a miraculous love like that of Florio and Biancifiore. If heeded, this love can change a life and reverse the erosion, both historical and personal, of *Romanitas* and Christianity.

4

Teseida I

The Fall of Arcita and the Failure of Pietas

LIKE THE *FILOSTRATO* OR *Filocolo, Teseida* is a work in which an event in the history of the pagan world is depicted in terms of the fundamental forces in human nature and human history that Christianity identifies. *Filostrato* shows how one kind of love and a disobedience to divine suggestion lead to personal and civic disaster. *Filocolo* shows the opposite: how a love that does not set itself apart from the divine leads to miraculous results, not just for individuals but for nations as well. *Teseida,* too, focuses on a great historical situation, the conquest of Thebes by Athens. In *Teseida,* Thebes comes to represent the libidinous aspect of man, and Athens, the human capacity for self-control, but the poem demonstrates the impossibility of such control in the absence of divine collaboration. In *Filostrato,* Troilus refuses to collaborate with deities closely linked to Christian Providence. In *Teseida,* however, pagan divinities are represented not as veiled figures of God's Providence but as demons. *Teseida* therefore shows the failure of human virtue, when it is not aided by grace, to exert control over human passions. It shows, in effect, the failure of pagan efforts to rule the irrational side of human nature and argues implicitly, therefore, for the necessity of Christian faith.

The story of Palemone and Arcita, two of the major protagonists in *Teseida,* is like that of Troilus. These men suffer the consequences of a dominating and ultimately destructive love. The *Teseida,* however, adds a further dimension to their story when it places Theseus over these men as ruler and as one who attempts to exert over them a control that they cannot manage. Theseus is a great man, relatively unmoved by passion, and willing to obey the gods, yet he fails to impose effective control on the lovers' behavior. His failure is not personal but lies in forces beyond his control. They are, as we will see, historical ones. Theseus's failure represents the failure of pagan men, even at their best, to impose control on man's fallen nature.

Neither *Filostrato* nor *Filocolo* hesitates to describe the behavior of pagan men and pagan communities in terms of Christian virtues. In these texts, Boccaccio treats such virtues as universally valid and sees them as at least potentially within the reach of men unenlightened by Christian revelation. In *Teseida* he turns away from this optimistic view, and, while he continues to maintain the universal validity of Christian truth, he depicts the inability of a pagan community, which is not itself vicious, to achieve the control of human passion. The reason for this failure is probably found in the historical situation of Athens. Both *Filostrato* and *Filocolo* depict events in the history of Rome that are linked by Vergil and Orosius to divinely sponsored destinies. The Athens of Theseus, however, is not part of this providential scheme. The face of divinity that Theseus encounters is not crypto-Christian and providential but ultimately satanic. Divorced from great actions in which God's Providence is at work, Theseus experiences the demonic dominance of human fate that governed the majority of mankind before the Incarnation. Theseus is a pagan whose individual efforts at goodness are thwarted by the historical and religious situation of the world in his era.

This more pessimistic theme is accompanied by a significant development in the way the ancient world is presented. It centers in Boccaccio's darker vision of the nature of pagan divinity. In the earlier poems I have discussed, Boccaccio represented the contact between men and gods primarily through dreams and epiphanies. In the *Teseida* contact with the gods, almost without exception, takes place within temples and is part of the normal course of pagan worship. Temples become the meeting place of men and gods, and that pattern, so characteristic of the heroic life, both in Boccaccio's earlier works and in Vergil's works, of direct and personal contact between men and gods, is for the most part absent in *Teseida*. Temples and related monuments embody the formal contact between worshiper and deity. Moreover, these structures are so placed in *Teseida* that they symbolize the development of Boccaccio's social and theological argument there. In effect, then, Boccaccio has made artifacts of the ancient world, which he has constructed with all the verisimilar skill at his command, the bearers of the thematic structure of his work. Ancient monuments serving their pagan religious purpose act as thematic signposts in the structure of a work about paganism. This is an extraordinarily successful means of connecting the larger historical situation with the conduct of individual life, for temples serve as the meeting points of cosmic and individual action. Not only the historical situation, then, but also the classicizing details of scene and setting carry out Boccaccio's argument in *Teseida.*

In this and the following chapter I will describe the shape of Boccaccio's argument in *Teseida* and the temples that punctuate his argument. I will describe the wilderness that occupies the middle of the poem and then sketch out the sequence of civic monuments that represent Athens's attempt to impose reason on savage men, the limited success of that attempt, and the divine settlement the city must finally accept. In the process I hope to reveal in *Teseida* a level of organization and sophistication that has not been observed and an integration, not achieved in the earlier poems I have discussed, of classical setting and action to produce a coherent argument about the limitations of historical paganism.

Critics have seen Boccaccio's *Teseida delle nozze d'Emilia* as the closest the poet ever came to harnessing the two forces always at play in his Neapolitan works.[1] On the one hand, the work is seen as classicizing, and Boccaccio is credited with a degree of erudition, especially in the glosses he composed to accompany the poem, that looks forward to his mature work of this type, the *Genealogies of the Pagan Gods.*[2] On the other hand, the work is clearly a romance, and, like *Filostrato* and *Filocolo,* it is patterned on French examples.[3] Critics have generally agreed that, while these two aspects of *Teseida* are both more skillfully carried off and more successfully integrated than in the other poems of this period, the blending of the love story of Palemone and Arcita with the martial themes of Theseus's success in battle and his clemency is, finally, imperfect.[4] The poem's own claim that it is "the first to sing of Mars in the Italian vernacular" (*Tes.* 12.84) and, as such, is entitled to membership in the epic tradition is generally not granted.[5]

Teseida is unified, however. From beginning to end it is, as the title suggests, a Thesead. Theseus is its central character, and the episodes in the poem represent a series of problems presented to him. In book 1, he faces the cruel and pitiless Amazons, whom he conquers. In the second book, he conquers the impious Creon. His motives in both cases are good ones, and his actions are effective. From each of these foreign campaigns he brings home prizes. From Scythia, the land of the Amazons, he brings his bride, Hippolyta, and her younger sister, Emilia. After conquering Creon, he leads in triumph the last survivors of the Theban royal house, Palemone and

Arcita. These living spoils of war, Emilia, Palemone, and Arcita, once they return to Athens, soon begin to interact: both Thebans fall in love with Emilia and so become increasingly savage rivals. Their interaction presents Theseus with a complex domestic crisis that is in effect an internalization of the conflicts he has resolved abroad by war. His efforts to control and direct at home the passions he has subordinated abroad, his failure to achieve this control, and his response as well as Athens's response to this failure make up the climax of the *Teseida*.

The plot of the poem is unified, then, although a combination or *contaminatio* of classical sources is recognizable in it. The imitative core of the poem is not the structure of Statius's *Thebaid* but its theme, the resolution by the godlike Theseus (with the collaboration of the gods and fate) of the civil and fratricidal war of the Seven against Thebes. Statius's poem is an indirect model, however; the last event in *Thebaid*, Theseus's decisive intervention against Creon, occurs very early in *Teseida*.[6] Boccaccio's poem is partly a continuation of the *Thebaid*, then, but it is also a response to it. He distances *Teseida* from Statius's poem by inverting the order of episodes in *Thebaid* and by inserting into it a partially disguised version of the second half of the *Aeneid*. From the moment Palemone and Arcita agree to fight for the love of Emilia, Boccaccio characterizes them, as I will show, as Aeneas and Turnus. Thus there are two Aeneases in the poem—the furious Palemone and the pious, self-controlled Theseus. Emilia, whose Latinate name recalls an Italian place-name, plays the part, both logically and explicitly, of Lavinia, Aeneas's Italian bride-to-be.[7] For the single combat Emilia's rivals have sworn, Theseus substitutes a more restricted form of combat. This duel breaks down, as does that between Aeneas and Turnus, and gives rise to a war in Theseus's amphitheater which is frequently punctuated with explicit references to the Italian warfare described in *Aeneid* 9–12. The gods finally intervene in the Athenian contest, as they do in the duel with Turnus, and force a result. This ends the Vergilian portion of the narrative, since the *Aeneid* itself ends with the death of Turnus. That much of the poem is described in this chapter. Boccaccio includes three more books, which I discuss in the following chapter.

The actions of these complexly intertwined Christian, Vergilian, and Statian plots take place within a landscape punctuated by a series of pagan monuments. Through the integration of these actions, rich in their reminiscences of Latin epic, and the monumental architecture of *Teseida,* a complex and far-reaching unity is achieved.

In the first book of *Teseida,* Theseus sets out to avenge the Amazons' murder of their husbands. Apparently fed up with masculine control, these women have rebelled and now rule themselves. Boccaccio's opinion of their action is unmistakable: it reveals them as "crude e dispietate" ["savage and without *pietas*"] (*Tes.* 1.6.2). By invoking the term "dispietate," Boccaccio seems to reflect its double sense, as lacking compassion on the one hand and negligent or irresponsible on the other. Theseus, who opposes them, is portrayed with increasing insistence as *pius.* Such a characterization, of course, suggests Aeneas, the "man outstanding for *pietas,*" as Vergil describes him (*Aen.* 1.10). Thus the confrontation between Theseus and the Amazons emerges as an essentially Vergilian conflict of almost emblematic quality, pitting cruelty and barbarism against Theseus's civilized virtues of compassion and responsibility.

The Amazons defend themselves with great strength and skill, and Theseus has the greatest difficulty making headway against them. Besieging them, he undermines their walls, and they at last recognize the impossibility of further resistance. They recognize at the same moment that their position is untenable not only physically but spiritually as well. Hippolyta sees the gods and not just Theseus opposing them (*Tes.* 1.116). Venus in particular, she believes, is their opponent; and the goddess has recruited Mars to aid Theseus (*Tes.* 1.117). When Theseus emerges as the victor, Hippolyta senses that he is not a cruel man. Indeed, he has the reputation of being "humble and easy to one who humbles himself" (*Tes.* 1.121, 4).

Moreover, in these portrayals by Hippolyta, Theseus comes to resemble Aeneas. He is supported by Venus, as Aeneas is. She sees him as one who also responds gently to those who are humble. This characteristic is one Aeneas is urged to adopt, although he cannot always achieve it. Anchises, as part of the procession of Roman descendants he shows his son, urges him "to impose the habit of peace, to spare the humble and to make war against the proud" (*Aen.* 6.852–53). There is no reason to be ashamed of submission to this man, as Hippolyta recognizes. Since the Amazons *are* women, there can be no shame in *acting* as women do (*Tes.* 1.121).

It is this recognition that finally makes the "natural" solution to the war possible. Theseus is a man, Hippolyta a woman; they can end their strife by marriage as well as by treaty, and this is what they both agree and desire to do. For their wedding, the temple of Venus, which the Amazon women had "serrato ne' lor primi mutamenti" ["barred up in their first rebellion"] (*Tes.* 1.134.3), is reopened, and a mass wedding ensues (*Tes.* 1.135). All the conditions of the Amazons' rebellion are reconciled by this wedding.

In this solution Theseus has emerged as a kind of Aeneas. He enforces the habit of peace by making war. He makes war to subdue the women who are *dispietate,* but he responds humbly to them when they humble themselves. He is championed by Mars for Venus's sake. As Aeneas aims to do but does not actually achieve in the *Aeneid,* he consolidates his victory by marrying his opponent. This marriage, like that projected for Aeneas, is carried out under the sponsorship of Venus.[8] She is represented not in person but by means of her Scythian temple. This temple becomes the first in the series of monuments that define the underlying argument of *Teseida.*

The victory over the Amazons is completed by a triumph not described until book 2. I anticipate the careful plotting of *Teseida* by describing the triumph here, but it is important to recognize that Venus does not stand alone. Her conquest of the Amazons is completed by and shared with the goddess Pallas, in whose honor the triumph is held. Immediately upon his return to Athens, Theseus

> diritto andò al tempio di Pallade
> a reverir di lei la deitade.
> Quivi con reverenza offerse molto,
> e le sue armi e l'altre conquistate
>
> [went straight to the temple of Pallas to worship her divinity. And there with reverence he offered much, both his own arms and conquered ones] (*Tes.* 2.23.7–24.2).

This donation of his own arms along with captured ones diminishes any sense of this as a triumph over the Amazons. Theseus triumphs with Hippolyta over the cruelty and pitilessness the Amazons had displayed. Similarly, the triumphant dedication to Pallas binds that goddess with Venus. It does not distinguish the two, and the reader may think of the whole triumph as one embracing Venus and Pallas. Such a fusion of deities has already occurred in

Filocolo. The image it suggests is wisdom in marriage or, in other common medieval terms, a union of reason and sensuality.[9] It is essential to realize, however, that despite their emblematic meaning, the goddesses are also to be understood as sponsoring divinities. The solution worked out through the collaboration of Theseus, Venus, Pallas, and ultimately Hippolyta is one that will prove impossible for men alone or for men in collaboration with the destructive face of pagan divinity to achieve.

Present at this triumph is Hippolyta's "sorella picciolina," Emilia (*Tes.* 1.128.6). She is too young for marriage, but Theseus reserves her in his mind for Achates (*Tes.* 1.137). Emilia has not taken part in the settlement by marriage of the Amazon problem. When she comes to Athens with Theseus, she remains a vestige of Scythia that will return to plague and ultimately defeat Theseus in the poem's crisis.

Palemone and Arcita, the men destined to be Emilia's suitors, are acquired by Theseus much as Emilia is. If anything, they are even more clearly spoils of war than she since they are captives; but all three become Theseus's responsibilities as a result of successful warfare. Their story begins in Scythia, where Theseus lingers after his marriage to Hippolyta. In a scene recalling the descent of Mercury to urge Aeneas's departure from Carthage, Theseus is confronted by a ghostly image of his friend Perithoos.[10] The image demands:

> Che fai tu ozioso
> con Ipolita in Scizia dimorando,
> sotto amore offuscando il tuo famoso nome?
>
> [What are you doing lazily staying with
> Hippolyta in Scythia, obscuring your
> famous name with love?] (*Tes.* 2.4.4–7).

While the apparition recalls the epiphany of Mercury in *Aeneid* 4, here, as is typically the case in *Teseida,* there is only indirect contact between man and god. When Theseus recovers from his fear of this sudden apparition, he realizes that

> dal cielo,
> da qualche deità la qual provede
> al suo onor con caritevol zelo,
> era venuto cotal ragionare

> [from the sky, from some deity
> who watches over his honor
> with loving zeal, this speech
> had come] (*Tes.* 2.7.5–7).

At the spur of this divine suggestion, Theseus, like Aeneas but unlike Troilus, obeys: he returns to Athens. In his absence the war of the Seven against Thebes has been completed.[11] That war, which is the subject of Statius's *Thebaid,* begins when Oedipus's twin sons contest their father's legacy. Each wishes to rule Thebes, and Polynices eventually raises an army incorporating seven Greek champions to fight for his rights. In a climactic duel, the brothers kill each other, and Jocasta's brother, Creon, assumes the Theban kingship. Creon, however, as Sophocles' *Antigone* describes, refuses burial to Polynices and the champions who fought at his side against Thebes. Their corpses are left to litter the ground outside the "liberated" city.

In this refusal of burial, Boccaccio sees evidence of "fiera crudeltà" ["savage cruelty"] (*Tes.* 2.12.7), worse even than that which characterized the Amazons. Also at issue in this war is behavior lacking in *pietas,* parallel to the Amazons *dispietate.* This aspect of Creon's behavior is reflected most clearly through those who enlist Theseus's help in fighting against him. These are Greek or Argive queens, the wives of the seven champions who fought alongside Polynices and to whom Creon also denies burial. As Theseus passes them on his triumphal entry into Athens, they urge him in the name of *pietas* to oppose Creon and ensure their husbands' burial.

The spot these women pick as vantage point while they wait to approach Theseus is significant. They choose the temple of Clementia, the deified personification of clemency. In placing the queens here, Boccaccio is following Statius, whose epic celebrates Theseus's triumphant exercise of this virtue. Boccaccio's point would seem to be a different one, however. He means to distinguish between the actions of Theseus's virtue that are in collaboration with divinity and those that are not. In book 2, as in book 1, Theseus opposes cruelty and impiety, and he does so under the tutelage of a divinity. In book 1, that divinity is represented by a combination of Venus and Pallas. Here it is represented by the divine Clementia. Like Venus's temple in Scythia, Clementia's temple stands for the collaboration between men and gods that makes Theseus's *pietas* effective.

The Argive queens see this virtue as primary, both in their own motivation and in Theseus's. "Pietose," they address Theseus as "pio signore" and ask that he be "pietoso" (*Tes.* 2.32.1, 2.32.5, 2.33.2). They define burial as the "pio oficio" (*Tes.* 2.34.3). Theseus himself identifies *pietas* as a motive for action. He is

> nella miseria delle sconsolate,
> da intima pietà nel cor trafitto
>
> [stricken to the heart with deepest compassion at the misery of the unconsoled] (*Tes.* 2.43.3–4).

He tells his soldiers,

> Certo ciascun ne dovrebbe esser pio,
> e al vengiar dovreste esser ferventi
>
> [Surely everyone must be compassionate, you must be eager to avenge] (*Tes.* 2.46.3–4).

Theseus's *pietas* is thus well established. His exhortation to his troops reaffirms his imitation of Aeneas's imperial responsibility:

> Andiamo adunque, e lui, fiero Creonte,
> umil facciàn con le spade tornare
>
> [Let us go there and make proud Creon humble with our swords] (*Tes.* 2.47.1–2).

Theseus is successful. His army overcomes Theban opposition, and he himself defeats Creon. Boccaccio's description of Creon's death directly recalls the death of Turnus.[12] Here that death is seen as justified, in contrast to the way it is viewed in *Filostrato,* and by it Theseus, like Aeneas, consolidates his victory over cruelty and lack of *pietas.*

Theseus clearly represents Aeneas throughout this book, and here he represents him at his most dutiful and successful: turning away from the distractions of Carthage and resuming his heroic responsibility; asserting his *pietas;* subduing cruelty in accordance with the Roman imperial mission. Every episode in the life of Aeneas that

Theseus's career recalls is a divinely sanctioned one of great importance, and Theseus's assumption of the perfected career of Aeneas is plainly established in books 1 and 2 of *Teseida.* In the remainder of the poem this Aeneas will confront himself in another guise, for, as I have already suggested, the trio of lovers and rivals who emerge from the first two books take on the roles of Aeneas, Turnus, and Lavinia. In effect, then, the poem pits a completed Aeneas against an incompleted one and lets the one attempt to set the other to rights. Before this can be achieved, however, two essential characters must be acquired at Theseus's charge.

At the death of Creon, Theseus gives Thebes into the hands of his men; they are to sack it at their pleasure, but the temples of the gods must remain inviolate (*Tes.* 2.73.6–7). Then follow the funerals of Creon and the Argive kings (*Tes.* 2.74–77). In a final act of vengeance, the Argive women burn Thebes itself (*Tes.* 2.81–88). Despite the multiple disasters and the repeated attempts by Thebes's enemies to kill its leaders and destroy its fabric—the last vestige of the crime of Oedipus—some spark of Thebes still remains. Theseus's men are ordered to search the battlefield, and there they discover

> due giovani feriti dolorando
>
> . . . . .
>
> e ciaschedun la morte domandava,
> tanto dolor del lor mal gli agravava
>
> [two wounded and sorrowful
> young men . . . and each asked
> for death, so much did sorrow for
> their misfortune afflict them] (*Tes.*
> 2.85.5.7–8).

When these two are led before Theseus, he asks them if they are members of the royal house of Cadmus.

> E l'un di loro altiero al suo dimando
> rispose: "In casa sua nati e cresciuti
> fummo, e de' suo' nepoti semo; e quando
> Creon contra di te l'empie arme prese,
> fummo con lui, co' nostri, a sue difese."
>
> [And one of them haughtily replied to
> his question: "In his house we were born

> and raised, and we are his grandchildren; and when Creon took up impious arms against you, we were with him, and with our own men in his defense"] (*Tes.* 2.88.5–8).

While Theseus is "aware of their disdain,"

> non seguio
> però l'effetto a cotale ira degno;
> ma verso lor più ne divenne pio.

> [the effect, however, appropriate to so much wrath did not follow, but he became more compassionate towards them] (*Tes.* 2.89.1–4).

Theseus and the Theban knights are thus strongly contrasted in this brief scene. The Thebans emerge from the most sweeping catastrophe almost as if by a miracle, and yet they retain the disdain and the wrath that first led to Thebes's disaster. Theseus does not respond to their wrath as he did to that of Creon but is merciful and keeps them alive for his triumph (*Tes.* 2.92.1–2). So he brings them into Athens before his chariot (*Tes.* 2.94–95), just as, in the triumph that begins book 2, he has brought Emilia to Athens. Theseus's second triumph in book 2 is a triumph of Mars: Creon's armor is dedicated in Mars's temple (*Tes.* 2.95).

Four monuments, then, focus and summarize the themes of the first two books of *Teseida:* the temple of Venus in Scythia and the temples of Pallas, Clementia, and Mars in Athens. Each is associated with a particular action, and each embodies significant themes in the poem. Each represents an aspect of Theseus's heroic character and, more significantly, an aspect of his successful imitation of Aeneas. The temple of Venus, where the marriage of Theseus and Hippolyta takes place, represents Theseus as Venus's champion and as one who responds to humility with gentleness. It represents the triumph of Anchises' formula for Roman imperialism and suggests the peace to be anticipated from the marriage of Aeneas and Lavinia. The temple of Pallas, the Athenian temple par excellence, complements the temple of Venus and characterizes the marriage of Theseus and Hippolyta as one in which sensuality and reason are blended. The temple of Clementia continues the imperial theme announced by Anchises, for clemency is both a private and an imperial virtue.[13] Here Theseus is presented with a task associated with *pietas* and is himself characterized as *pius*. He sets out to make war against the proud, and, like Aeneas, he is victorious. That wrathful victory is rightly celebrated in the temple of Mars. This triumph, however, like that preceding it, is one combining the virtues of contrasting gods. Venus associated with Pallas blends reason and sensuality. Mars associated with Clementia suggests wrath tempered by compassion. While Theseus defers his virtue to these paired divinities, his success is unparalleled.

This is the pinnacle of Theseus's achievement and the high point of his imitation of Aeneas. After this point in the poem, Theseus is no longer alone in representing Vergil's hero. At the moment of their enamorment, both Palemone and Arcita reflect elements of Aeneas's character, and later in the poem they assume Vergilian roles that overlap those Theseus continues to play. From a window of the prison where Theseus perpetually guards them, Arcita one morning sees the Amazon Emilia. In wonder, he exclaims, "Quest' è di paradiso!" ["She is from Paradise!"] (*Tes.* 3.12.8). He invites Palemone to join him at the window and tells him, "Vener è qui discesa veramente" ["Venus has in truth descended here"] (*Tes.* 3.13.3). Palemone is equally certain that this vision is celestial, and he identifies the unknown girl with the same goddess: "Per certo questa è Citerea" ["Certainly this is Venus"] (*Tes.* 3.14.6).

The Thebans thus mistake Emilia for Venus. While there are no direct verbal resemblances, the scene in many of its themes reflects Aeneas's meeting with his mother in Carthage and the work the goddess and Cupid carry out there.[14] When Aeneas first sees Venus in disguise he recognizes her divinity but cannot identify her. This scene at first glance seems an odd model for an enamorment, but its main motif, the identification of the girl with a goddess, reflects both its Vergilian origin and a major theme in Boccaccio's notion of love. Boccaccio often represents the act of falling in or out of love as one in which divinity plays a part. Typically, enamorment involves the recognition of a divinity—usually Cupid or Amor—in some earthly woman. To the extent that the earthly woman is seen in terms of divinity, the love remains exalted. When divinity is ignored and the woman is loved for herself alone, the love then becomes problematical. Troilus experiences this debasement of a love that is divine in its origins. Here the love of Palemone and Arcita for Emilia begins on the same exalted level.[15]

The Venus who appears in Emilia certainly has her origin in the *Aeneid;* but, unlike the Venus who aided Theseus against the Amazons, she is revealed in the end as a destructive force. Robert Hollander has argued for a substitution of Venuses at the beginning of book 3 of *Teseida.*[16] In his view, whereas the Venus who sponsors Theseus's war against the Amazons may be thought of as the celestial Venus, as her association with Hymen and Pallas argues, here a furious and predatory Venus has appeared. It is true that Theseus reacts differently to Venus's suggestion than these Thebans do. Nonetheless, it is not so much their desire that distinguishes them as the way they respond to their own passion. Theseus has some discipline and self-control; the Thebans have demonstrated none. When an impulse as strong as love strikes such different people, the results are bound to be different.[17]

While the way love affects them is exceedingly important, Theseus's eventual inability to control the passion of the Thebans reflects the fact that love is, in Boccaccio's view, always divine in origin. In their fury, Palemone and Arcita are still collaborating with an aspect of Venus. Theseus, in opposing them, is not collaborating with any god or goddess. Instead, he sets himself and his own virtue against the will of the gods. Even though this may seem to be a confrontation between his good and the gods' evil, what emerges is not a victory for the good but a demonstration of Theseus's impotence in the face of divine opposition. Theseus's impotence, moreover, is shared by all men unaided by divinity in their struggle against the irrational forces in human nature. This, as I will argue, is the underlying theme of *Teseida.*

The sparks of love first struck by the celestial image of Emilia quickly become threatening when the freed Arcita, who has assumed the name of Penteo (Pentheus) and returned to Athens, encounters his former cellmate, Palemone, who is newly escaped from prison. The two meet not far from Athens in a grove, or bosk (*bosco* or *boschetto*), where Penteo has often gone:

> E era sì rimoto da l'andare
> di ciaschedun, che ben poteva il foco
> d'amor con voci fuor lasciare andare

[And it was so remote from the path
of anyone that the fire of love could
be released in words] (*Tes.* 4.64.3–5).

The grove is a little paradise, and Boccaccio describes it in the conventional terms appropriate to a *locus amoenus* (*Tes.* 4.65).[18] It serves as the scene of the decisive actions in the middle books of *Teseida.* Its fate becomes tied more and more closely to that of the lovers, and, as their passions become less restrained, they cause it increasing damage. Finally, at the death of Arcita, it is felled to make space for his funeral pyre. Thus its fate is like the fate of paradise, from which it conventionally descends. It is gradually involved in the destructive play of human passions and suffers death as a consequence of human actions.

The bosk is the complement to the monuments that dominate the enclosing portions of the poem. It reflects the opposition between Theseus's civilizing virtue, *pietas,* and the cruel, even bestial opponents who resist him. While its biblical resonances are manifest, it recalls with equal insistence the involvement of the Italian landscape in the fury of the war in Italy described in *Aeneid* 7–12.[19]

The first encounter of the lovers in the bosk is distinctly one-sided. Arcita is asleep, and Palemone, the eventual winner of Emilia, the man who will soon be figured as Aeneas, and the aggressor in this encounter, addresses his sleeping cousin in imagination:

O bello amico molto da lodare,
se al presente tu ti risentisse,
tosto fra noi credo si finirebbe
qual di noi due per donna Emilia avrebbe

[O lovely friend greatly to be praised,
if at present you were to awaken I think
that soon between us would be de-
cided which of the two of us would have
Emilia for his lady] (*Tes.* 5.36.5–8).

Arcita awakens:

E'nsieme si fer festa di buon core
e i loro accidenti si narraro

> [And they greeted each other wholeheartedly and told each other their adventures] (*Tes.* 5.39.1–2).

This good spirit remains until Palemone asks Arcita to give up his love for Emilia and let her be his alone (*Tes.* 5.40.3–4). Arcita is enraged at this, and Palemone expresses surprise that his cousin will not yield (*Tes.* 5.41.1–4). It is Palemone, however, who presses for battle and Arcita who resists (*Tes.* 5.43.1–3). Palemone swears a battle oath:

> Io ti giuro, per l'onipotente
> Giove del cielo e per Venere dea,
> che prima ch'io di qui faccia partenza,
> co' ferri partirén tal differenza
>
> [I swear to you by the omnipotent Jove of the heavens and by the goddess Venus, that before I leave here this dispute will be settled with swords] (*Tes.* 5.43.5–8).

This oath is based on one Aeneas makes at a critical point in the *Aeneid.*[20] In the second half of that poem, Aeneas, although he has reached Italy, must fight to secure his foothold in that country and to win his promised bride. His opponent, Turnus, who thinks of Lavinia as pledged to him, raises Italian tribes against Aeneas and his Greek ally. After heavy losses on both sides, Aeneas and Turnus agree to end the war by single combat. To give their decision the force of law, representatives of the two contending forces meet and swear treaty oaths. Palemone's oath reflects that sworn by Aeneas. Arcita eventually swears an oath as well, but first he acknowledges that this battle is not their own entirely but is brought about by the will of the gods:

> Omè, ch'io sento l'ira dell'iddii,
> li quali ancor ne vanno minacciando
> contrarii tutti alli nostri disii;
> e la fortuna ci ha qui lusingando
> menati con effetti lieti e pii,

> e non Amore, a voler che moiamo
> per le man nostre, come noi sogliamo.
> Omè, che m'era assai maravigliosa
> cosa a pensar che Iunon ci lasciasse
> nostra vita menare in tanta posa,
> e come i nostri noi non stimolasse

> [O how I feel the wrath of the gods who still threaten us, all of them contrary to our wishes; and deceptive Fortune has led us here and not Love, with happy and pious results, wishing that we would die at our own hands, as we are accustomed to do. O how marvelous a thing it appeared to me that Juno would let us live our lives in such quiet, and would not goad us as she did our fathers] (*Tes.* 5.55.2–56.4).

Arcita's complaint, then, widens the context of the lovers' rivalry. It is not entirely of their own making but bears with it the heavy weight of Thebes's heritage, the divine wrath of Juno and the fratricide that often springs from it. This Theban theme emerges parenthetically, however, from an essentially Vergilian scene, and the goddess it identifies as the enemy of Thebes is a vindictive presence in the *Aeneid,* too.[21] While Palemone has called on Jove and Venus in his oath, Arcita refers to Juno, not as his patron but as his destroyer. Turnus, the champion Arcita will soon recall, is the favorite of Juno. She stirs the Italian champion to resist the invading army led by Aeneas, knowing full well that Aeneas is supported not only by her rival Venus but also by omnipotent Jove and the will of fate. Her action in stirring Turnus to futile and ultimately fatal resistance is thus an irresponsible and cruel one. It only delays the fated victory of Aeneas, but it leads to Turnus's death. When Arcita recalls Juno, then, not as his patroness but as his destroyer, he is telling a truth about himself as Turnus, which Turnus never realizes. Juno destroys both Arcita and Turnus, one through "friendship," the other through enmity, but when the gods are involved (as Dido and Aeneas learn to their cost), contact itself is often fatal.[22]

As political leader, Latinus, the father of Aeneas's eventual bride, swears an oath that will govern Turnus in his fight with the Trojan. Arcita's vow, like this Vergilian counterpart, is a moving pastoral lament. He uses his oath, in fact, to express not his animosity but his unwillingness to do battle. He calls on all the elements of nature, the sky, the rising sun, the unnamed sylvan deities, and Priapus, not as a god of lust but of orchards, as Boccaccio's own gloss makes clear.[23] Like Turnus, Arcita is closely bound to the earth and to the natural world, and his oath reflects this. Arcita and Turnus are natural men; here, before battle, at their most dignified and restrained, they speak for a compelling sympathy among men and between man and nature.[24] When this sympathy is overcome by wrath, they become victims, and so too does the pastoral world they represent.

Battle soon begins, but not before the knights are offered an opportunity to reconsider their violent course of action. No sooner has the fight begun than

> il valoroso Arcita
> su l'elmo con la spada a Palemone
> diede un tal colpo ch'appena la vita
> li rimanesse fu sua oppinione
>
> [the valorous Arcita gave such a
> strong blow with his sword to
> the helmet of Palemone that he
> thought life could hardly remain in
> him] (*Tes.* 5.66.1–4).

Arcita's reaction fits his earlier reluctance; he "wept in sorrow" ("piangeva doloroso"); he regrets his blow and the love that led to it (*Tes.* 5.70.2, 5.70.8). Meanwhile, Palemone comes to. He realizes that Arcita is weeping for him (*Tes.* 5.72.7–8), but he nevertheless insists that battle resume:

> Non creder però aver perdono
> da me, perché pietoso t'ho veduto
>
> [But do not think to be excused
> by me because I have seen you
> compassionate] (*Tes.* 5.73.5–6).

These are the familiar Vergilian terms that have distinguished opponents in previous confrontations in the *Teseida.* Arcita, like

Theseus, is *pius,* but this virtue, in strong contrast to its effectiveness in the earlier books of the poem, is here both short-lived and impotent. Bestial wrath soon overwhelms it, and both Thebans begin to "ferir come draconi" ["wound each other like dragons"] (*Tes.* 5.75.8). The simile recalls the origin of the Thebans, who were sown from the dragon's teeth "sanza aver più l'un dell'altro pietate" ["without having any more pity for each other"] (*Tes.* 5.76.3).[25]

While the Theban rivals are hard at their destructive task, Emilia, who has become separated from a hunting party led by Theseus, happens into the bosk. She is the very image of Diana.

> Ell'era sopra d'un bel pallafreno
> co' can dintorno, e un corno dallato
> avea e dalla man contraria al freno,
> dietro alle spalle, un arco avea legato
> e un turcasso di saette pieno,
> che era d'oro tratto lavorato;
> e ghirlandetta di frondi novelle
> copriva le sue treccie bionde e belle
>
> [She was on a beautiful palfrey with dogs around her, and she had a horn, and at the side opposite her bridle hand, behind her back, she had a bow tied and a quiver full of arrows which was embroidered with gold threads; and a garland of new branches covered her blonde and beautiful tresses] (*Tes.* 5.79).

Though the scene has medieval elements, it also recalls the hunt in *Aeneid* 4; and the description of Emilia has a great deal in common with the description of Dido before the hunt that leads to her false "marriage" with Aeneas and to her eventual death (*Aen.* 4.129–39).[26] Her effect on the two combatants is most Dido-like. She inspires them not to virginal coldness but to an increased ardor. At the sight of her, both warriors become "più forti e più fieri" ["stronger and more fierce"] (*Tes.* 5.80.6). For them this becomes a second enamorment. It is not so much a falling into love as a falling into *furor* that expresses itself in combat. Because their wrath is now fed by the very vision that established love and mutuality before, from this moment on, the love of Palemone and Arcita for the same woman is an impossibility.

Theseus soon follows Emilia into the bosk, and, once there, he parts the combatants. Learning who they are, he acknowledges, as they do, their violations of his law, but he determines to pardon them. This pardon is superficially like the role the more formal virtue of pardon, clemency, has already played in the poem. Clementia, from whose temple precincts the Argive queens appeal to Theseus for their husbands' burial, is a divinized, imperial virtue. Theseus's march against Creon, which begins in her temple, enjoys the sponsorship of that divinity. His success in overcoming the bestial cruelty of Creon is at least partially attributable to the goddess. Here, Theseus's action in pardoning the Thebans is different in motivation and in kind. It is based on the recollection of his own experiences: Theseus was once in love, and it led him to acts as risky and extreme as those the Thebans have carried out. As Boccaccio's gloss explains, "In his youth Theseus abducted Helen, daughter of Tindarus, who was later stolen away by Paris; but Theseus's mother returned her to Castor and Pollux, her brothers, without her ever having been touched by Theseus: for this reason his offense was pardoned."[27]

Acting on the basis of his own experience, Theseus gladly pardons the errant Thebans. This is not an official act but a personal one, not a divinely instigated act of clemency but an example of individual mercy. There is nothing wrong with such an act, as long as its limitations are understood. However, Theseus appears to disregard these limitations, and his merciful act runs counter to those divinities whose interest in the love and combat of the Thebans has already been manifested. In effect, then, Theseus's intention to be merciful runs counter to fate and to the divine will. We cannot expect it to succeed in the way his earlier, divinely sponsored actions did.

Theseus asserts more than mercy in this scene. He declares, as the lovers have earlier declared themselves, that *pietas* will be opposed to their fury. This, too, is a familiar opposition in the poem, but once again, the opposition is made in terms that do not fully correspond to the pattern of *Teseida* 1 and 2. There, *pietas* embraced Theseus's devotion and duty to the gods. Here, it is an individual, perhaps civic, characteristic or virtue. Although it is not wrong to assert *pietas,* then, the virtue is impotent without divine response. We saw it quickly evaporate when Arcita tried to assert it single-handedly early in the duel with Palemone. It is not immediately set aside or overpowered in the poem's final books, but it nevertheless fails.

Theseus sets his *pietas* against the lover's passion in a single, highly important statement. He asserts, "Vincerà il fallo la mia gran pietate" ["My great *pietas* will overcome their fault"] (*Tes.* 5.92.8). Theseus's assertion that his *pietas* will overcome not only the *furor* of the knights but also their *fallo* is an extremely bold one. In the poem's climax it will prove to be impossible. No man, not even Theseus, can set his will against love. Love is a god who collaborates with human will; he is not to be overturned by a man alone, even a man whose *pietas* is as great as that of Theseus. Moreover, the love of these men and their Theban fate has a demonic dimension that will become clear in the poem's denouement. Theseus unaided by grace has no power to oppose its force.

Theseus's method for overcoming this "fault" is to remove the combatants from the wilderness and to impose order on their combat. He sees regulated battle as the only way to settle their dispute. He regards that as a rather pleasant and amicable thing, calling it "amorosa battaglia" (*Tes.* 7.8.1), and relies on a monumental amphitheater in Athens as the proper setting for imposing order on the unregulated *furor* of the Theban barons.

This theater eventually replaces the grove and signals the reemergence in the poem of urban monuments like those that governed in books 1 and 2. It represents the imposition of civilized Athenian control on the unregulated practices of the wilderness. It represents, too, the monument by which Theseus proposes to exert the control of his *pietas* over the lovers' fault. In book 6 of the *Teseida,* however, we hear little of this monument, and it does not yet serve as a scene for the action of the poem, a role in which it will dominate for much of the second half of *Teseida.*

Book 6, instead, is entirely occupied with an extensive description of the champions each Theban assembles in his behalf. Far from being an intrusion into the structure of the poem, the book carries on the poem's themes of *furor* and *pietas.* It anticipates the contest in the theater when it introduces those who will take part in it. More significantly, it introduces an analogy, which is also present in Vergil and Statius, between war and games. This analogy, like the identities of the warriors who take part in the contest, suggests the impossibility of controlling *furor* in the way that Theseus intends to do. Just as the amorous battle at Troy leads to massive destruction, destruction that is recalled in the war in Italy, and just as Thebes itself has been decimated by the Argive army, so Theseus's theater is about to be overthrown by the combined fury of the champions of these past and future battles.

The proximate source of book 6 is the description in *Thebaid* 2 of the Argive champions, but the combatants in Theseus's theater include heroes who play prominent roles in the war in Italy, whose coming together is described in *Aeneid* 7, and others clearly associated with the Trojan War.[28] This is a rather ominous beginning to a game, accenting as it does both the martial and fratricidal elements of two of the struggles it recalls and the libidinous cause of the third. It also serves as a prelude to the particular nature of the bloody contest in Theseus's theater.[29] There, as we will see, the wilderness reemerges not as a physical setting but in similes describing the savagery of the combatants and more particularly in a series of scenes directly recalling significant battle deaths in *Aeneid* 9–12 and *Thebaid* 7–10.

The list of champions begins with Lycurgus, "ancora lagrimoso / per la morte d'Ofelte, a ner vestito" ["still weeping for the death of Opheltes, dressed in black"] (*Tes.* 6.14.1–2). His appearance as the first of the champions epitomizes the themes I have already described, but with an ominous emphasis. Opheltes' death is the occasion for the games that, in *Thebaid* 6, stand before and forecast the war of the Seven against Thebes. In the *Teseida* Opheltes' funeral is systematically recalled in the funeral of Arcita. Lycurgus's entrance as Arcita's champion, then, foreshadows the doom that will befall that hero.

The champions Agamemnon and Menelaus (*Tes.* 6.21–24) recall the Trojan War. Their companions in arms, Castor and Pollux, are described in relation to their sisters, Helen and Clytemnaestra, the one responsible for the destruction of Troy and the other, of Argos (*Tes.* 6.25). All four champions thus recall the war that serves as the very model of *amorosa battaglia.* The war to avenge Helen's rape by Paris symbolizes, both in Latin poetry and in Boccaccio's *Filostrato,* the martial *furor* love can produce. Boccaccio blends these champions with those described in the second half of the *Aeneid.* The systematic reference to the *Iliad* in the second half of that poem anticipates this conflation.[30]

Other Greek champions include Pelleus, Chromis, Hippodamus,

Nestor (who takes no part in the war against Thebes), Perithoos, Ulysses and Diomedes, Admetus, Anchelados, and several others. Of these, Admetus, Chromis, and Hippodamus participate not only in the war but in the funeral games for Opheltes as well.[31] Pelleus is a famous though unscrupulous racer himself. Ulysses and Diomedes, who have no place in the *Thebaid*, are champions of the Trojan War and two who stand in Vergil's poem for the worst of Greek treachery and cruelty. At the time of the Theban War, Nestor, although he was of appropriate age, "refused to take part in a doomed campaign."[32] As Vessey points out, this "traditional exemplum of wisdom has no part in folly."[33] Despite his wisdom, however, Nestor plays a role in Theseus's game. Evander is similar. His age, wisdom, and *pietas* mark him off and make his participation in the war in Italy inappropriate. Nevertheless, he enters this tragic contest.

Perhaps the most interesting and surprising champions to enter the theater are Pygmalion and Sychaeus. Sychaeus is the husband of Dido, and she had vowed to him her eternal chastity. He is thus a reminder of the violation of her vow and her chastity which love for Aeneas represents. Pygmalion is the murderer of Sychaeus.[34] The appearance of Pygmalion and Sychaeus together here naturally recalls what happened between them. The two are united by bonds of kinship, yet Pygmalion, in *furor* and *impietas*, disregarding his sister's affection and moved by a lust for gold, destroys his companion. The story has some of the dimensions of the story of Palemone and Arcita, of course. Their tie is blood and not marriage, yet *furor* divides them, too, and the killing of one by the other would be a kind of fratricide, the Theban crime par excellence and an example of horrid *impietas*. That Dido stands between Pygmalion and Sychaeus as Emilia, a Dido figure, stands between Palemone and Arcita is also suggested by their presence here.

I have described elsewhere the disposition of the theater and its archaeological and ideological functions.[35] It is Theseus's monumental response to the unregulated *furor* of the Theban barons, who meet in fratricidal battle in the bosk outside Athens. Theseus himself emphasizes the benign nature of the contest in the theater: there is, he says, no kingdom at stake here, no disputed heritage (*Tes.* 7.7.3–5). He emphasizes, too, the consanguinity of the Argive people and the inappropriateness of bloodshed among father, son, and other close relatives (*Tes.* 7.10.4–7). To avoid the consequences of such actions and given what he believes to be the benign nature of the strife between Palemone and Arcita, he imposes a number of conditions on the battle. These conditions justify, he feels, his belief that the contest will be not like a war but "com'un palestral gioco" ["like a wrestling match"] (*Tes.* 7.4.8). This game, moreover, will not win, as a fratricidal war would do, the hatred of the gods (*Tes.* 7.10.5); instead,

> Questo sarà come un giuoco a Marte,
> li sacrifici del qual celebriamo
> il giorno dato; e vederassi l'arte
> di menar l'armi in che c'esercitiamo
>
> [This will be like a game to Mars,
> whose sacrifices we celebrate on the
> given day; and the art of bearing
> arms, in which we exert ourselves,
> will be displayed] (*Tes.* 7.13.1–4).

In at least two matters Theseus is seriously deluding himself. As the catalog of champions has already shown, the strife provoked by love is no less than that provoked by lost kingdoms or inheritances. Agamemnon and Menelaus fight to regain Helen; Paris and his nation fight to keep her. Theseus has seen these very champions "d'affanno d'ira e d'amor pieni assai" ["filled with fatigue, wrath, and love"] (*Tes.* 7.11.8). Yet, despite what he has seen, he believes that the "amorosa . . . battaglia" in his theater will be relatively harmless. He believes, too, in the efficacy of his own *pietas* and of his own capacity to regulate so much *furor.*

Theseus recognizes the presence of another force in the theater as well, and just as he misunderstands the fury of the human combatants there, he also misapprehends the power and malevolence of this second presence. Mars acts in the theater; his sacrifices are celebrated on the appointed day of battle, and in effect this game will be dedicated to him. As I have shown elsewhere, Boccaccio was familiar with Roman games dedicated to Mars.[36] Like the contest in the theater, they are far from benign or bloodless. Mars, too, of course, is the god of war, and his presence in the theater as dedicatee of the games is another reminder of the analogy between game and war. When the game escapes Theseus's control, two factors will combine to make it do so. The *furor* of the lovers, which he underestimates, and the power of the god, which he appears to regard benignly, will combine to overthrow his *pietas* and sabotage his plans.

In addition to the theater, three significant monuments emerge in the seventh book of *Teseida.* These are the temples of Mars, Venus, and Diana, where the lovers and Emilia express their devotion to patron gods and make the prayers that determine their fates. Arcita expresses his devotion first, and it is directed primarily toward Mars. Palemone's prayer to Venus is in keeping with his portrayal in the earlier oath-swearing scene as Aeneas, another hero championed by the goddess. Emilia, as a former Amazon and still a virgin, prays to Diana. There has been considerable discussion of the temples, the deities they enshrine, and the elaborate glosses Boccaccio provides to their mythographical and allegorical significance.[17] My aim is to establish the notion that these temples, like the theater and like the temples of *Teseida* I and 2, are monuments that center and embody the meaning of Boccaccio's poem. All the participants in the conflict leading up to Arcita's death are represented by these monuments: Venus and Mars, who oversee the contest, are each represented by a temple; Diana, too, has a shrine. Theseus's *pietas* is represented by the theater itself. This configuration of monuments recalls the similar configuration in books I and 2. There, temples of Mars and Venus were also present, but no human institution was set against or among them. The temple of Clementia and the temple of Pallas, instead, stood as monuments that supported Theseus's *pietas* and his assumption of the imperial task of Aeneas. Here that *pietas* is unsupported by divinity, as the solitary theater suggests.

In its imagery and in many of its details, the battle in Theseus's theater is, as the catalog of heroes has forecast, not a game but a war. Its civilized setting, moreover, is transformed by *furor* into a wilderness. In it the gods participate, as they regularly do in battles, and in the end the outcome there is determined by their choice in collaboration with the fallen will of men.

The human savagery that transforms the game into war and the theater into a wilderness is apparent in the similes introducing the major combatants. Arcita enters first:

> Tale a veder qual tra giovenchi giunge
> non armati di corna il fier leone
> libico, e affamato i denti munge
> con la sua lingua e aguzza l'unghione,

e col capo alto, quale innanzi punge,
l'occhio girando, fa dilibrazione;
e sì negli atti si mostra rabbioso,
ch'ogni giovenco fa di sé dottoso

[In appearance like the savage Libyan lion when it comes among heifers not yet armed with horns, and famished, licks [lit., milks] its teeth with its tongue and sharpens its claws; and with its head high and rolling its eyes, it deliberates which to strike first, and it shows itself by its acts to be so enraged that each heifer is terrified of it] (*Tes.* 7.115).

The savagery of the lion, his predatory deliberation, the contrast between his strength and the weakness of his domesticated prey, even the implied Libyan setting, all combine to show that Arcita is far from embodying the constraints of the civilized contest he has entered.

Palemone is described in similar terms, but the epic simile following his entrance into the theater refers specifically to the bosk where the lovers first did battle. In the simile it has been transformed from a *locus amoenus* into a wild and savage place:

Qual per lo bosco il cinghiar ruvinoso,
poi c'ha di dietro a sé sentiti i cani,
con le sete levate e isquamoso,
or qual or là per viottoli strani
rugghiando va fuggendo furioso,
rami rompendo e schiantando silvani,
cotale entrò mirabilmente armato
Palemone

[As through the bosk the destructive boar, when it has heard the hounds behind it, with its bristles raised and shaggy, wandering this way and that runs through strange paths fleeing, furiously breaking branches and de-

> stroying the woods, so Palemone
> entered wonderfully armed] (*Tes.*
> 7.119).

The simile clearly suggests that the bosk, a place where hares and rabbits were hunted with dogs and snare, is now the scene of a savage boar hunt and that in fleeing the hounds the boar causes it considerable harm. The savagery of the boar, which represents the savagery of Palemone, continues the process of destruction which his wrath began. It is significant, too, that, as Limentani recognizes, this simile is at least loosely based on *Aeneid* 10.707–13.[38] There it is applied to the savage Mezentius as he stands in for Turnus. In Palemone's career as Aeneas, this is a surprising substitution. However, it is characteristic of the *furor* of battle in the second half of the *Aeneid* that men of such different natures as the civilized Aeneas and the barbarous Mezentius act in similar ways.[39] The simile thus reflects again the relationship between the games in the theater and the war in Italy.

Deaths occur in the games as they do in the war, and their very existence gives evidence of the failure of *pietas* to control the action there. Some of these deaths are modeled on death scenes in the *Aeneid* and *Thebaid,* and such recollections reinforce the already well established deterioration of the game into a war. Two scenes in particular recall a climactic moment in the career of Aeneas when his own *pietas* is overcome by *furor.* When Turnus kills Pallas, whose father, Evander, has placed the young hero under Aeneas's protection, the Trojan hero appears to go berserk. Possessed by unmatchable *furor,* he rages through the battlefield and slaughters every enemy in his path. He single-handedly chases the Latin forces from the field (*Aen.* 10.510–605). He kills violently and without mercy. His fury is first recalled in *Teseida* when the champion Artifilo Itoneo kills Cremiso:

> E mentre lui lo suo fratel pio
> volea levar, li sopragiunse il forte
> Eleno, e orgoglioso il perseguio
> e lui uccise ancor similemente
> allato al frate dolorosamente
>
> [And while in compassion he
> tries to lift his brother, the

strong Helenus came up to him
and arrogantly attacked and
killed him, too, miserably at
the side of his brother] (*Tes.*
8.15.4–8).

The details recall Aeneas's brutal killing of two brothers as they fight to protect each other (*Aen.* 10.335–41). A similarly poignant battle death from *Aeneid* 10 is recalled later in book 8. This time, Arcita is the killer, and his victim, his face clotted with blood, calls out:

Se te padre raspetasse,
Quale hai me concio qui ti ritrovasse

[If indeed a father waits for you,
may that which you have done to me
find you out] (*Tes.* 8.84.7–8).

This scene, as Limentani notes, is loosely based on one in which a Latin soldier begs Aeneas for mercy (*Aen.* 10.597–98).[40] The plea is unsuccessful.

A savagery like that Aeneas shows in his rage at Pallas's death transforms Theseus's urban theater into a war zone. This process is further abetted by the gods. Mars and Venus, unlike the human spectators in the theater, look on at this scene of human violence and are dissatisfied. Mars especially senses "intiepidire il foco / che facea prima gli animi ferventi" ["that the fires were cooling that earlier had made hearts burn"] (*Tes.* 8.112.3–4). To rekindle this ardor, Mars, taking the form of Theseus, appears in the theater and berates Arcita (*Tes.* 8.112). The effect of the god's appearance is decisive. Their wrath rekindled, Arcita and his companions move against Palemone and his men, who "alquanto nel cor paurosi / divenner" ["became somewhat fearful at heart"] (*Tes.* 8.117.3–4). Shortly after this intervention, Arcita's faction is victorious when Palemone is seized by the man-eating horse of Cromis.[41]

Theseus, the constant emblem of *pietas* in the first two books of *Teseida* and the man who asserts the dominance of that virtue in this very struggle, does not actually take part in the fighting. Nevertheless, even he is not immune to the *furor* manifested in the theater. Although Theseus remains in his seat, he is nonetheless

tutto nel viso rosso come foco,
tanto 'l disio del combatter poteo,
di che più volte si tenne per poco

[all red as fire in the face, so powerful was the desire for combat from which several times he barely restrained himself] (*Tes.* 8.89.3–6).

As a spectator, Theseus, too, capitulates in the triumph of *furor* over *pietas.*

Every factor, then combines to transform the theater of Theseus into a scene of savagery and furor. Although it is urban and man-made, it is transformed by human passions into a wilderness of violence. By the same process, the game Theseus designs for it becomes a war. The gods themselves aid this process, entering the theater and enflaming one group of champions against the other. Even Theseus succumbs to the pull of rage. Finally, it is the gods who determine the outcome of what Theseus expected to control himself. Their conclusion is the final and most blatant triumph of fury over *pietas.*

From above the acropolis, the gods look down on the scene in the theater (*Tes.* 9.2).[42] They are content with the way events have worked out so far, they see a chance to fulfill the prayers of their worshipers. Arcita, the worshiper of Mars, has won the military victory for which he had prayed. Palemone has prayed to Venus not for victory but for Emilia to be his, and now the goddess prepares to reward her worshiper, as she explains to the war god:

Bene hai d'Arcita piena l'orazione,
che, come vedi, va vittorioso;
or resta a me quella di Palemone,
il qual perdente vedi star doglioso,
a mio poter mandare a secuzione

[You have completely fulfilled Arcita's prayer; he is, as you see, victorious; now that of Palemone, the loser, who is miserable, as you see, remains for me to bring to completion as best I can] (*Tes.* 9.3.1–5).

The particular method Venus chooses to achieve her goal confirms the triumph of *furor* over *pietas,* already evident in so many ways. Venus has already visited hell, where she has chosen one of the Furies, here called Erinis, for her purpose.[43] The Fury, whose terrible form is described at length (*Tes.* 9.6), appears in the theater in the poem's only epiphany and causes great horror. The Fury's appearance, which is strongly reminiscent of manifestations of the divine in *Filostrato* and especially in *Filocolo,* shocks even the elements and the building itself (*Tes.* 9.6.5–8). The terrifying figure causes Arcita's horse to rear, and the beast falls on its rider. In this fall Arcita is mortally wounded (*Tes.* 9.8).

Arcita's fall from his horse completes the ordering of events that Venus and Mars have worked out between them to fulfill their worshipers' prayers. Arcita has the victory he prayed for, and the way is now cleared, after his lingering death, for Palemone to have Emilia. With the intervention of the Fury, too, the work of *furor* itself is completed. Theseus's *pietas* could not prevent the death of Arcita or, as it quickly appears, the deaths of fourteen other champions in the theater game. Theseus was indeed wrong when he asserted, "Vincerà il fallo la mia gran pietate." The *furor* of man's nature and the gods' collaboration with it have overcome Theseus's unaided virtue.

In his death fall, Arcita resembles Mezentius, as Limentani notes. At the conclusion of the contest in the theater, this identification of Arcita with one of Turnus's strongest and most furious companions in arms is significant. The confusion in the theater, which was reflected in the identification of both champions with Mezentius and Aeneas, appears to have resolved itself. In his fall, Arcita again resembles the furious Latin opponents of Aeneas. This general identification is given extra weight and extra significance by an event that quickly follows. Seeing the fall of the man she has immediately regarded as her fiancé, Emilia laments:

> Ora conosco ciò che volea dire
> Bellona sanguinosa, che davanti
> oggi m'è stata

> [Now I understand the significance of Bellona who has stood before me all day covered with blood] (*Tes.* 9.12.1–3).

This description recalls the angry prediction of Juno as she surveys the effects of Aeneas's campaign in Italy. She promises Lavinia, the presumed fiancée of Turnus who will eventually be won by Aeneas, that the goddess of war will be her bridesmaid:

> Sanguine Troiana et Rutulo dotabere, virgo
> et Bellona manet te pronuba
>
> [You will be dowered with the blood of the Trojans and Rutulians, virgin, and Bellona will go before you as bridesmaid] (*Aen.* 7.318–19).

By identifying Emilia with Lavinia, the equation between the contending suitors, Palemone and Arcita, and their Vergilian equivalents, Turnus and Aeneas, is reinforced.

The dying Arcita is identified with yet another Vergilian hero. After he is pulled from under his horse and laid in the theater, he soon regains consciousness. He cannot speak,

> ma gli occhi erranti in qua e 'n là voltava
> or questo or quello con sembianza pia
> mirando
>
> [but he turned his wandering eyes here and there, looking now at this one, now at that with a pitiful gaze] (*Tes.* 9.17.3–5).

Boccaccio's specification that Arcita's gaze went "here and there" ties the passage directly to a significant moment in the *Aeneid.* When Dido becomes convinced that Aeneas will indeed abandon her, her tender mood and expression change:

> Talia dicentem iamdudum aversa tuetur
> huc illuc volvens oculos totumque pererrat
> luminibus tacitis et sic accensa profatur
>
> [She had been looking at him distractedly while he spoke; then turning her gaze here and there, and looking him up and down, with empty eyes, and altogether enraged she spoke] (*Aen.* 4.362–64).

It is this empty look of incomprehension, not the rage that follows, that Arcita shares with Dido. He shares her tragic fate as well. She is as much a victim of her passion and the treachery of Venus, which aroused it, as she is Aeneas's victim. With this final portrayal of Arcita, his characterization becomes comprehensible and complete. He represents Turnus, Mezentius, and Dido, victims of Aeneas and of their own *furor* and victims of the gods as well.[44] Dido, the victim of Venus, Mezentius, the victim of Jupiter, and Turnus, the victim of his protector, Juno, are merged in Arcita, whose fall, like theirs, is caused by *furor* in collaboration with an ultimately malevolent divine will.

In terms of the monuments of *Teseida,* then, it is clear that the temple of Venus, where Palemone makes his prayer, the temple of Mars, where Arcita prays, and the temple of Diana, where Emilia expresses her devotion, overpower the theater that stands for Theseus's unaided *pietas.* This is true, but the situation is more complex. I have suggested elsewhere that the theater is not a neutral structure or one that represents paganism in an unambiguous fashion.[45] On the one hand, the theater is a monumental architectural achievement, and it testifies to the wealth and social organization of the ancient world. However, the theater also shows, as the Christian fathers asserted, the fundamental depravity of pagan culture. It is the theater, scene of bloody hunts, lewd plays, and violent gladiatorial contests, that shows most powerfully the uncontrollable passions of pre-Christian society. In a very real historical sense, the theater represents the *furor*—either lascivious or violent—that Roman culture, despite the civilizing mission Vergil announces, continued to reflect. The theater as the scene of Theseus's attempt to calm the *furor* of Palemone and Arcita is therefore a prejudiced choice. Christian, indeed, Stoic, polemic has paved the way for the notion that theatrical shows represent not *pietas* by any means but massive inducements to every sort of libidinous excess.

It is equally significant that the ancient theater was not a secular institution. Theseus may presume to rule there and pretend to impose order on the events that occur there, but, as the Christian encyclopedist, Isidore of Seville, summarizing a long tradition, continually asserts, theaters and theatrical games were dedicated to the pagan gods, and simple attendance at their functions constituted idolatry and demon worship.[46] The intervention of the gods is to be anticipated, then, for the theaters are dedicated to their cult. The particular form in which the divine enters the theater in *Teseida*—that is, through the infernal if not the blatantly demonic—is predicted by the encyclopedic tradition of the Christian Middle Ages, as it is by patristic literature.

Theseus's choice of the theater as the scene for the confrontation of Palemone and Arcita is thus not just a misfortune within the context of the poem; it is, in a very real sense, historically determined. The institution Theseus chooses for the resolution of his problem is fundamentally corrupt. It fosters *furor,* not *pietas,* and it invites the intervention of gods who are really demons. In essence, then, Theseus's failure is not merely a private one; it also has implications for the whole of paganism. In Boccaccio's view, neither Athens nor the pre-Christian world in general can assert the control of *pietas* over *furor.*

Boccaccio uses this theater not only to assert this failure of historical paganism but also to critique major themes of the *Aeneid* and *Thebaid* from a Christian point of view. Both of these poems concern themselves with the control of *furor* by *pietas.* Generally speaking, Boccaccio sees the *Aeneid* as the story of Aeneas's attempt to assert control over his own violent and libidinous nature and that of his antagonists. Such control is only ambiguously reflected by the final event of the poem, Aeneas's furious killing of Turnus. It is clear, however, that where such control does occur, it occurs with divine sanction, and it is continually aided by the pacification of furious divinity by Jupiter and fate. In the *Thebaid,* there is a clearer triumph of *pietas.* There, Theseus, aided by fate and divinity, achieves a final settlement of Theban *furor.* That settlement had eluded Adrastus, a hero who was good and *pius,* as Theseus is, but never found his efforts seconded by divinity. Adrastus was right in his views, but he was ineffectual because his will was out of touch with the gods. Theseus's *pietas* prevails not only because of his greater personal qualities but also because his intervention in the aftermath of the Theban War is divinely supported. It is the purpose of *Teseida,* too, to assert the importance of the divine in overcoming *furor.* When the divine cooperates with *pietas, furor* is put down. When divinity is contrary, human effort is unavailing. While these themes are implicit in both the *Aeneid* and the *Thebaid,* Boccaccio makes them explicit and uses them to make a statement about pre-Christian society.

It is essential to this argument that the pagan gods in the second half of *Teseida* are not figures for Christian Providence. As Orosius argues, certain actions of the pagan gods were indeed providential. As I have argued in the case of the *Filocolo,* Boccaccio sees Providence at work in many moments of history. He sees it principally in the historical events that led to the founding of Rome, which, in its appointed time, gave birth to and disseminated the gospel of Christ. Not every action of the pagan gods is providential, however. The majority, while not contrary to the will of God, will certainly serve the more immediate ends of those demons who have presented themselves, in the Christian polemical view, to the credulous as Venus, Mars, Juno, and the rest. This is precisely what Theseus experiences. The gods who intervene in his theater are demonic in their manifestations and have little inclination for aiding his pious intentions.

We can ascribe to Boccaccio in *Teseida,* then, a critique of paganism. He asserts in general that *furor* cannot be controlled by *pietas,* not only because passion overcomes man's self-control but also because the divine that should aid man is, in the days before Christ, largely demonic. The pagan claim to control *furor* through *pietas* is contradicted here. Without Christian or providential divinity to second it, Boccaccio argues, *pietas* is insufficient.

In the aftermath of this failure, the whole of Athenian society expresses its overpowering grief through an elaborate funeral and through unrestrained mourning. Then begins a series of monumental responses to Arcita's death which emphasizes the role of art and virtue in a world no longer innocent of death.

5

Teseida 2

After the Fall: Fame, Monuments, and Marriage

THE FAILURE OF THE CONTEST in the theater and the death of Arcita mark a significant turning point in *Teseida.* Before these occurrences, Theseus's confidence and his ability have not been seriously tested. Here they are overcome. His unaided *pietas* was not able to oppose the "fault" of Palemone and Arcita. Indeed, his *pietas* barely restrained his own wrath. In the aftermath of the failure, Theseus, Athens, and the lovers mourn Arcita so intensely that their grief, bordering on despair, threatens to overwhelm them all. The failure of *pietas* and the destruction of hope are evident in the monuments that replace the theater and the temples of the gods, and around these the action of *Teseida* refocuses. The first "monument" is a funeral pyre built for the fourteen champions who lose their lives in Theseus's "wrestling match." The second and more significant is the pyre of Arcita himself, which is built in the bosk where he first gave expression to the flames of his love. This pyre is answered by two things: one is a monument pure and simple, the historiated tomb Palemone builds for his fallen comrade; the other, equally classicizing but more intangible, is the sequence of highly suggestive prizes offered to the victors in Arcita's funeral games. The first monument represents the triumph of death within historical pagan culture and within a tradition of reading pagan poetry literally. The second, through its adducement of allegories of the virtues, implies a spiritual response that redeems pagan culture, not in itself but for Boccaccio's Christian reader.

These monuments are all associated with the long and elaborate funeral of Arcita. This funeral is closely modeled on one described in the sixth book of the *Thebaid,* but Boccaccio makes significant changes.[1] Some of these are archaeological in inspiration, but most are thematic. In this extensive episode, however, Boccaccio so completely integrates imitation of ancient epic and reconstruction of an ancient monument that it is impossible to separate them. The book becomes a repossession, to the fullest extent Boccaccio ever encompasses, of his classical and epic heritage. It repositions *Teseida* within a sequence of monuments whose very historicity suggests the temporal and spiritual limits of pagan culture.

The funeral of Arcita is the third funeral described in *Teseida*. It follows the funeral of the Argive kings who died fighting before Thebes and the funeral of the heroes who die in Theseus's theater.[2] In both cases, these funerals move closer to the mainstream of action in the poem. They begin with kings who never figure in the poem as living men; they then pass to fourteen champions who participate in the central contest in the theater; finally, they involve one of the principal characters in the poem. This increasing centrality of the funerals to the plot of the poem is reflected in the increasing length and elaboration of each account: the funeral of the Argive kings is described in a few lines; the funeral of the champions of the theater is recounted in a number of octaves; the funeral of Arcita, however, requires almost the whole of the eleventh book of *Teseida*.

The preparations for the funeral begin with Theseus's command that the bosk where Arcita first sang of his love be cut to provide space for his pyre.[3] After the grove has been leveled, an enormous pyre is built. Boccaccio compares its height, in a simile that has no counterpart in *Thebaid*, to the giants' work in piling Ossa on Pelion:

> Poco più furo i monti accumulati
> sopra Tesaglia dalla folle gente,
> inverso il ciel mattamente elevati
> che fosse quivi quel rogo eminente
>
> [The mountains piled up above
> Thessaly, insanely raised up
> toward the sky by the mad race
> [of Titans], were little higher than
> this pyre] (*Tes.* 11.26.3–6).

This enormous pyre gives monumental form to the funeral of Arcita, and it joins the succession of temples and other buildings that have symbolized the themes of earlier books. The pyre responds most directly to the theater; it is there that Arcita receives his death wound. The height of the pyre recalls as it exceeds that of the theater, where the high marble walls seem "to wear out the eye" (*Tes.* 7.108.4–7). In a figurative sense it resembles the theater, too. The giants set Ossa on Pelion in an attempt to equal Olympus; Theseus's theater is set against the temples of the gods and their mansions. Though his motive is pious, unlike the giants', his opposition, like theirs, ends in disaster; and the pyre monumentalizes Theseus's failure.

The description of the funeral blends historical details with repeated evidence of the triumph of death over Theseus's *pietas*. As Roman funerary custom requires, Theseus places a gift on the corpse of Arcita; the gift, however, not only signifies his feeling for the Theban but becomes a sign of abdication and failure:

> E acciò che Teseo intero segno
> di nobil sangue desse di costui,
> tutti vi fé gli ornamenti da regno
> venir presenti, e adornarne lui;
> lì le veste purpuree, con ingegno
> fatte, si videro addosso a colui;
> lo scettro e 'l pomo e l'eccelsa corona
> per lui al fuoco del suo rogo dona
>
> [And so that Theseus might give a full token of the noble blood of this man, he had all the ornaments of the kingdom brought, and adorned him with them; there the purple vestments woven with skill were seen worn by him, the scepter and the orb and the high crown for his sake he gave to the fire of the pyre] (*Tes.* 11.36).

This extravagant gift is anticipated in Statius, where King Lycurgus, whose only son, Opheltes, lies dead, is the donor: "At genitor sceptrique decus cultusque Tonantis / inicit ipse rogis" ["But the father himself threw onto the pyre his beautiful scepter and signs of his priesthood of Jove"] (*Theb.* 6.193–94).

In anger and despair, he consigns his regalia to the pyre, "si damnis rabidum queat exaturare dolorem" ["as if by this condemnation he might satisfy his raging grief"] (*Theb.* 6.83). He throws the fillets he wears as priest of Jove upon his son's pyre, too (*Theb.* 6.193–94). This is a violent and impious gesture. It is worthy of the furious kings who contend at Thebes. Theseus's imitation of it, especially given the dispassionate spirit that Boccaccio portrays, is chilling. Theseus's is not an act of rage but a self-conscious act of despair. It is a deliberate destruction of the emblems of his authority in the aftermath of his failure in the theater. Boccaccio makes further use of the tragic grief of Lycurgus. Not only does Theseus mimic him in dedicating his regalia; Palemone, Emilia, and the Athenian crowd all reflect aspects of the king's impious rage. His inconsolable grief, in fact, comes to characterize the response of all Athens to Arcita's loss.

Arcita's bier is finally lifted onto the shoulders of the "best of the Greeks," and the *pompa,* or funeral procession, begins. Following bearers of sacrifices and offerings comes the bier itself,

> e con esso d'Attene usciron fori,
> con alto pianto la gente gridando,
> l'iniqui idii e li loro errori
> con alte voci spesso bestemiando
>
> [and with it the people came out
> of Athens shouting, and with
> loud voices cursing the wicked
> gods and their shortcomings]
> (*Tes.* 11.38.3–6).

This tumultuous scene, too, is something of a pastiche from Statius. Its core is the brief passage in which the bier of Opheltes, like that of Arcita, is borne in procession:

> Longo post tempore surgit
> colla super iuvenum—numero dux legerat
> omni—ipse fero clamore torus
>
> [A long time afterward the bier is brought
> up on the shoulders of young men—
> the leader has chosen them from all his
> number—with a furious clamor] (*Theb.*
> 6.128–30).

The noise that the procession makes, described by Statius in two words, "fero clamore," is greatly embellished by Boccaccio. Boccaccio represents this traditional noisiness, a common feature of Roman funerals, in an unusual way.[4] The noise is produced not only by cries, shouts, and sobs, but by curses as well, and these curses are directed against the gods.[5] In this way Boccaccio parcels out some of Lycurgus's violence and blasphemy among the crowd, and their outrage reflects a general dismay over Arcita's death. All of Athens is prey to despair in its aftermath.

The crowd is out of control in action as well as words, and this is apparent in their behavior at the deposition of the bier,

> la qual fu tosto dalla gente spessa
> che li seguiva tutta intorniata,
> per ciò veder, con disoluta pressa
>
> [which was quickly surrounded
> by the thick crowd that had fol-
> lowed in an unregulated bunch
> to see it] (*Tes.* 11.39.4–6).

This, too, depends on a scene in *Thebaid*, but it is a revealing inversion of the original. In Statius the bier is indeed surrounded by a crowd, but one comprising a disciplined band of soldiers whose job is to block the view of the pyre: "Optentis eminus armis / prospectu visus interclusere nefasto" ["And from a distance with their weapons they shut off sight of the unholy prospect"] (*Theb.* 6.204–5).

Their action, like their attitude, is the very opposite of that of Boccaccio's crowd.[6] Simple soldiers, they serve to restrain the passions of kings and queens; in this they reflect the emotional polarities that often exist in tragedy between unmoved chorus and maddened hero. In Boccaccio's scheme of things, however, this disparity is reversed: the despairing calm of Theseus contrasts with the boisterous mourning of the whole Greek people, represented by the crowd of warriors and townspeople.

Boccaccio's account continues to reflect details of Statius's poem, but it continues also to refer these activities away from one central mourning figure. Emilia brings the torch to Arcita's pyre, and after a short eulogy she lights it (*Tes.* 11.39). Statius associates this task with Lycurgus. Although the king does not carry it out, its performance is signaled by the end of his bitter invocation to Jove (*Theb.* 6.203). Boccaccio's assignment of this action to Emilia is an appropriate one. From his first falling in love with her, Arcita has been consumed by the flames of passion. Those flames have finally brought him to his death. It is fitting, therefore, that Emilia, who first inspired these metaphorical flames, should be the one to bring them to life and to set them to their final task.

Another of Lycurgus's mourning gestures is assigned to Arcita's cousin and rival.

> Palemone s'avea
> la barba e' crin tutti quanti tagliati
> e posti sopra Arcita e sì dicea
> con sommo pianto: "O iddii spietati,
> con altro patto certo mi credea
> che questi crini vi fosser litati;
> ma poi nell'are, iddii, non li volete,
> nelle dolenti esequie li prendete"
>
> [Palemone had cut his beard and his hair, and placed them on Arcita, and he said with a great sob: "O pitiless gods, with another vow, I thought these locks would certainly be sacrificed; but because you do not want them at that altar, take them at these sad obsequies"] (*Tes.* 11.47).

This passage represents the content but not the tone of an impassioned and defiant address to Jupiter, in which Lycurgus casts off his ceremonial fillets and places them, along with his hair and scepter, on his son's corpse:

> Alio tibi, perfide, pacto,
> Iuppiter, hunc crinem voti reus ante dicaram,
> si pariter viridis nati libare dedisses
> ad tua templa genas, sed non ratus ore sacerdos,
> damnataeque preces; ferat haec, quae dignior, umbra
>
> [With another intention, treacherous Jupiter, did I, swearing a vow, devote this hair to you, if you in return would grant that in adolescence my son might pour out libations in your temple, but this was not ratified by the priest and the prayer was doomed. Let this shade who is worthier bear them] (*Theb.* 6.197–201).

Palemone's action lacks some of the ceremonial exactitude and the shocking details of Lycurgus's speech.[7] Lycurgus has been "voti reus," the technical term for one who is under an obligation imposed by a vow. Throwing the hair he has pledged to Jupiter on his son's bier is not just a conventional gesture, then, but, like most of the king's mourning acts, it reflects his rage at the god who has disappointed him so cruelly. None of this is seen in Palemone. He is disappointed, but he offers to the dead an appropriate gift, a gift he would have offered at the wedding altar had the gods agreed. In Palemone's imitation of Lycurgus's action, however, Boccaccio extends his portrayal of grief at Arcita's death until that grief involves every figure in the poem.

Boccaccio's painstaking portrait of an ancient funeral and his generalized portrayal of the grief that Arcita's death inspires dramatically show the failure of Theseus's contest. At this most classicizing moment of the poem, we are confronted with the central problem of paganism as a Christian poet saw it: that is, the impossibility of combating the forces in human nature and in the demonic world that lead men to death. *Pietas* cannot overcome man's *fallo*—not just his *furor,* but his fallen human nature—from which fury springs. Only Christianity promises eternal life to the faithful.

Such a dichotomy between a pagan and a Christian point of view is presented in the poem's two responses to Arcita's death. One of these is monumental in the literal sense, the other is allegorical. The monumental gives rise to the poem's final pagan response—consolation in the face of death. The figurative monument suggests a response that the Christian reader, unlike the pagan actor, can, with the aid of faith, put to effective use.

The pagan theme of consolation is embodied in the elaborate tomb Palemone constructs to hold Arcita's remains. It is a *heroon,* a combination tomb and shrine, and its details reflect elements of the temple-tomb of Opheltes in *Thebaid* 6 as well as those of the temple in Carthage where Dido first encounters Aeneas.[8] Like the Carthaginian temple, it is dedicated to the goddess Juno.

If it were not for this dedication, Arcita's temple-tomb would be archaeologically unimpeachable. A temple-tomb, however, would be dedicated not to any Olympian god but only to the *manes,* or spirit, of the dead.[9] As a dedicatee for a funerary temple, Juno is inappropriate; indeed, even as a patron for a historiated temple, she is unnecessary, since Opheltes' own temple-tomb, as Statius describes it, is decorated with sculpted or painted scenes (*Theb.* 6.242–48). Boccaccio has no archaeological reason for calling up this temple from *Aeneid* 1.

He has an excellent thematic reason for doing so, however, and it is this that lies behind his reference to Juno in Arcita's tomb. In discussing why Emilia lights Arcita's pyre, I suggested that since passion for her had led to his death, the flame that consumed his body might most appropriately be brought by her. A similar theme is present here. That temple in Carthage is, like the temple where Troilus and Criseida meet in Troy, the setting where the doomed love of Aeneas and Dido conventionally begins in the readings of the Middle Ages. Because of this the temple comes to symbolize the beginning of a disastrous love.[10] It is appropriate, then, that at Arcita's death, this temple of love's initiation should be merged with the temple-tomb. The temple of Juno in Carthage is cast again as the temple of love that leads through wrath to death, and as such it is the most fitting spot for Arcita's burial.

An even more interesting manipulation of his sources is found in the stories that Boccaccio places on this temple. The temple-tomb of Opheltes is decorated with the story of his death. The panels on the temple of Juno tell the story of Troy's fall. Boccaccio has his temple tell Arcita's story, which is, of course, appropriate, but he does so in a curious way. The Trojan stories on Juno's temple in Carthage do not repeat narrative that has already taken place in the *Aeneid;* instead, they fill in the background of the story. The death of Opheltes is narrated in the *Thebaid,* but the temple images do not resume it at great length. Boccaccio, on the contrary, summarizes not just the tale of Arcita but the whole of *Teseida.* While this may appear redundant, it serves two important purposes. It provides a résumé of the poem and thus prepares for its conclusion in book 12. It has a more important thematic effect, however, for it ties the whole of the *Teseida,* as it is epitomized here, to the death of Arcita. In effect, it makes the whole of *Teseida* an *ekphrasis* on the tomb of that hero. Symbolically, therefore, Boccaccio's whole poem becomes an extended narration on a tomb. It becomes an epitaph and a lament for loss. In this way it shares all of Athenian society's reaction to the hero's death. Like Athens, the poem itself, as it is monumentally represented here, mourns the irrevocable loss of Arcita.

This tomb is not the only response to Arcita's death, however, and elegy is not the poem's final self-definition. A series of historiated objects, prizes offered in the funeral games for Arcita, responds to that death as well. The stories illustrated on them offer a different response to death and counterpoise the temple-tomb as monument of defeat.

Although emblematic objects are a common feature of late medieval poetry, such prizes and especially the project of including ancient games in a medieval poem are unprecedented, difficult, and very ambitious. The technical requirements of some ancient games are complex and continue to vex scholars, whose evidence includes the epigraphy, archaeology, and iconography unknown to Boccaccio. Boccaccio's predecessors, the authors of the French romances of chivalry, had not made this attempt.[11] Boccaccio, however, includes only ancient games in his poem and attempts the difficult task of describing them in his glosses.

Vergil and Statius, the primary epic models for *Teseida,* carefully work their games into the fabric of their poems. Both use them to reflect on the horrible realities of war.[12] In *Teseida* 6, Boccaccio has used the catalog of heroes to suggest such a war game analogy, and here he uses the games to different effect. By accentuating the prizes rather than the contests, he emphasizes the emblematic and not the physical; and so in his poem the prizes in his games play a role analogous to the role that the games themselves play in the structure of his models.

The first game celebrated at the funeral of Arcita is a footrace. There is no description of the race itself. The winners are simply named, but their prize is described in great detail.[13] The victors, "Ida e Castore," who have tied, each receive a prize:

> Per premio del valore un dono caro:
> ciò fu per uno un caval covertato
> di nobili coverte, u' si mostraro
> da uom, d'ingegno altissimo dotato,
> di Pallade gli onor, quando pigliaro
> nome novello i Cicropi, e ancora
> v'era il palude ove pria fé dimora.
> Vedeasi ancor le fistule sonare,
> le quali ella trovò primieramente;
> poi con Aragne folle disputare,
> e di Vulcan vi si vedea vincente
>
> [A rich gift as reward for his valor:
> that was, for each, a horse covered

> with a rich covering, where was depicted, by a man endowed with highest talent, the honors of Pallas. (First was shown the time) when the Cecropians took a new name; and then there was the lake where she first lived; there you could see her playing the pipes which she first discovered; and then see her dispute with Arachne, and you might see her victorious over Vulcan] (*Tes.* 11.60.2–61.4).

The victor's prize, described at such length here, has no exact correspondent in either Statius or Vergil. It represents a conflation of several passages in Latin poetry. In Vergil many prizes are assigned in the footrace, but none is historiated.[14] In Statius a horse is given to the victor, but its coverings, if any, are not described (*Theb.* 6.644–45). In Statius's chariot race, however, a prize that in some sense resembles this one in *Teseida* is awarded. Amphiaraus, the winner of that race, receives a wine-mixing bowl, or *crater*, on which is depicted the battle of the centaurs and Lapiths (*Theb.* 6.531–39). Hercules is prominently featured on the bowl, and, indeed, he formerly used it "seu monstri victor seu Marte" ["whenever he was victorious over a monster or in battle"] (*Theb.* 6.534). The second prize in Statius's chariot race is a cloak with the story of Hero and Leander embroidered on it (*Theb.* 6.540–47). Boccaccio appears to have combined the horse, the cloak, and the historiated *crater* in a single prize. The scenes that are depicted on the horse cloth are derived not from Statius or Vergil, however, but from Ovid. In the Arachne episode of the *Metamorphoses*, as I will describe in detail, there is an ancient precedent not for a prize but, nevertheless, for a historiated woven cloth with scenes from the life of the goddess Pallas.[15]

Statius's historiated prizes, and especially his association of this prize with Hercules, are of great importance for understanding the emblematic prizes of *Teseida*. Hercules is an important figure in the *Thebaid*. He is a champion both in games and in war. Generally speaking, his figure contrasts with the warriors at Thebes and the participants in Statius's games. They are more like Hercules' opponents, the centaurs, who, as Vessey has argued, "in the *Thebaid* symbolize the bestial, useless madness that drives men to war."[16] Hercules stands aloof from them as a representative of semidivine valor controlled and set to proper uses.[17]

Unlike those in which Hercules takes part, the stories told about Pallas are not accounts of valor against furious men or monsters. They are, instead, stories of the discovery of various arts and the victory over passion. Nevertheless, they play an emblematic role in *Teseida* like the one Vessey observes in Statius's Hercules. The cloth depicting scenes from the legend of Pallas shows the arts that can best respond to Arcita's death and serve as antidotes to the *furor* that caused it. As such they are spiritual counterweights to the historiated temple-tomb of Arcita, providing hope where that monument suggests only despair.

The first scene on the cloth depicts the naming of the Athenians. According to the poem, we are to understand that the Cecropians changed their name in honor of the goddess.[18] This appears to be a change of identity, not just a change of name. According to Eusebius, Cecrops "first of all called upon Jove, invented idols, an altar, and sacrificed victims; never before had things of this kind been seen in Greece."[19] Cecrops, then, is the originator of idolatry.[20] When the Cecropians change their name, this may suggest a transformation from idolaters to lovers of wisdom or truth.

The next scene on the cloth shows the lake, Tritonis, where Pallas first lived. Boccaccio's gloss to the poem assigns the lake little significance in itself but identifies it as the scene of important discoveries: "In Asia è una palude, la quale si chiama Tritone, dove una vergine, chiamata Minerva, primieramente abitò, e quivi trovò l'arte del filare la lana e di tessere i panni. Questa Minerva e Pallade sono una medesima, e fu poi questa Pallade da quello padule [sic] dove prima abitò chiamata Tritonia" ["In Asia there is a lake called Tritonis, where a virgin called Minerva first lived and there discovered the art of spinning wool and weaving cloth. This Minerva and Pallas are one and the same, and since then this Pallas has been called Tritonia from that lake where she first lived"] (*ad Tes.* 11.60.8). This lake is thus the scene of Minerva's invention of weaving and spinning and her conferring of these arts on mankind.[21]

The next scene recalls Pallas, still residing near Lake Tritonis, as the inventor of another beneficial art:

> Dicono alcuni che questa Minerva, cioè Pallas, dimorando allato alla soprascritta palude, delle cannuccie, le quali nascevano nella

palude, primieramente compose le sampogne. Altri dicono che, poi che i giganti furono vinti e uccisi dagl'iddii e li loro corpi furono consumati dalla terra, che, essendo sole l'ossa rimase, avvenne un dì che Pallade vide per uno osso stato di gamba entrare il vento, e sentì che uscendone sufolava; di che ella il prese, e, agiuntovi alcune cose, ne fece una sampogna: e da questo ebbero le sampogne il primo cominciamento

[Some people say that this Minerva, that is, Pallas, living on the shores of that lake, first made pipes from the reeds that grew in the lake. Others say that, after the giants had been conquered and killed by the gods and their bodies consumed by the earth with only the bones remaining, it happened that Pallas one day saw the wind enter a leg bone and heard it as it came out make a whistling sound. For this reason she took it, and having added some things to it, she made it into a pipe and from this pipes had their origin] (*ad Tes.* 11.61.1).

Pallas is being credited here with the invention of an instrument Boccaccio is calling a *fistula*. The *fistula* is a set of panpipes, and its origin is attributed to Minerva in Ovid's *Fasti.*[22] One-half of Boccaccio's story of its origin seems directly appropriate to that instrument, but the other half does not. Reeds might well compose a *fistula*, but the thigh bones of giants would hardly serve. These bones recall the Titans, however, and in the context of this book, that recollection looks back to the pyre of Arcita, which is compared to the Titans' work (*Tes.* 11.26.3–6). Minerva appears here to have formed from the Titans' destruction an instrument that makes music. Perhaps it is not too farfetched to suggest that in *Teseida* such music is a direct response to the failure the funeral pyre represents.

Music was regarded not as an idle form of amusement in the Middle Ages, but as an art of both great usefulness and great intellectual significance.[23] Praises of music were common; a beautiful one is found in Isidore's *Etymologies:*

Without music no art can be perfect, nothing indeed without it. For the world itself is thought to be composed by a harmony of sounds, and the sky to revolve to the modulation of harmony. Music moves passion and provokes the senses in several ways. In battle the harmony of the trumpets inflames the warriors, and by however much more vehement the noise becomes, by that much more is their spirit fortified for battle. Even oarsmen are urged on by song. Music softens the spirit and makes it more able to tolerate suffering. The fatigue of every labor is eased by the harmony of the voice. Music calms excited minds, as we read of David, who by the art of harmony took Saul from the grasp of an impure spirit. The beasts themselves, even serpents, birds, and dolphins, music calls to listen to her melodies. And whatever we say, or if we are moved by the pulses of our veins themselves, through musical rhythms and by the forces of harmony it is clear we are bound together.[24]

Music is a universal art, as Isidore sees it; not only men but also the earth, heavens, and animals are all moved by it. To men particularly it brings a variety of benefits. It arouses the passions or cools them as need be. Its greatest accomplishment, however, appears to be the aid music brings to man in sustaining daily suffering and in confronting the difficulties of work. The necessity of labor and endurance of the suffering labor brings is one of the primary conditions of the post-Edenic world.[25] Music is an art that helps to lessen this fundamental human hardship.

The next scene depicted on the cloth is the well-known dispute between Pallas and Arachne. Boccaccio's gloss explains this story as well:

Aragne fu una giovane di bassa condizione, la quale fu ottima maestra di tessere, intanto che ella osava vantarsi d'esserne migliore maestra che Pallade; laonde Pallade, presa forma d'una vecchierella, andò a lei e cominciolla amichevolemente a riprendere, dicendole che ella non faceva saviamente di volersi agguagliare agl' iddii, non che farsi maggiore. Di che Aragne le disse villania; onde Pallade subitamente si trasformò nella sua vera forma e dissele se ella voleva tessere a pruova con lei. Aragne, vergonandosi d'essersi vantata e non ritenere lo 'nvito fatto da Pallas, disse di sì. Fece adunque ciascuna di loro la sua tela: quella di Pallas fu più bella; il che veggiendo Aragne per dolore s'impiccò per la gola; ma Pallade non sofferse ch'ella morisse, anzi la convertì in ragnolo, il quale, non avendo la sua arte dimenticata, ancora tesse come noi veggiamo

[Arachne was a young girl of low estate who was an accomplished weaver, so much so that she dared to boast herself a

> better mistress of her art than Pallas. So Pallas, having taken the form of an old woman, went to her and started to reprove her in a friendly way, telling her that she was not acting wisely in wishing to set herself equal to the gods, let alone in setting herself above them. For this Arachne reviled her. At that, Pallas suddenly transformed herself into her true form and asked her if she wished to compete at weaving with her. Arachne, ashamed to have boasted and not to accept the challenge of Pallas, said yes. Each one made her cloth. Pallas's was the more beautiful. When Arachne saw that, she hanged herself by the neck in her unhappiness, but Pallas did not permit her to die, instead, she changed her into a spider which, without having forgotten her art, continues to weave, as we see] (*ad Tes.* 11.61.3).

This long gloss emphasizes the great importance Boccaccio attached to the stories he only alludes to in his text. The story of Arachne is in any case extremely well known and was widely retold in antiquity and the Middle Ages. Its most compelling version is certainly that in Ovid's *Metamorphoses,* and Boccaccio's gloss seems to reflect that account. Nevertheless, Boccaccio differs from Ovid in one important particular. In Ovid's poem the workmanship of the girl and the goddess are equal: "Non illud Pallas, non illud carpere Livor / possit opus" ["Not Pallas, not Envy herself could fault that work"] (*Met.* 6.129–30).

This comment has led William S. Anderson to conclude, "Ovid seems to suggest that Minerva, both as artist and as spiteful female, could find no fault with Arachne's artistic opus."[26] Boccaccio simply asserts, however, that "Pallas's was the more beautiful tapestry." This deviation from Ovid's text simplifies an otherwise difficult episode and makes Boccaccio's emblematic use of the story clear. If Ovid were not the poet he is, we would expect the goddess's skill to surpass the girl's, but it does not, and, like a sore loser, Minerva destroys her rival's work. Anderson finds this unfair, but it is arguable that skill in representation is not the only standard by which a depiction of the gods should be judged. The benefits Minerva confers on mankind, which are depicted on her cloth but not on Arachne's, may be thought of as justifying her victory.

Both Arachne's weaving and Pallas's weaving share themes with Ovid's poem. Both weavers tell stories about the loves and labors of the gods, and this is the central theme of Ovid's poem. It may be, then, that the cloth of Pallas and that of Arachne are representations within the *Metamorphoses* of two possible visions of that poem. If we see the *Metamorphoses* in Arachne's terms (as it appears to be commonly viewed), it seems to mock the gods and describe only their amatory excesses. If we see it in terms of Pallas's cloth, it is a celebration of the gods and their power and of the good they confer on mankind.

By stating that Pallas's cloth is more beautiful, Boccaccio has apparently indicated his choice of the goddess's vision. In so doing, I believe, he is offering a reading of his own poem in a way that is analogous to Ovid's. Since Minerva is shown as patroness of the arts and as goddess of wisdom, her story is an appropriate context in which to present this model. Before turning to that theme, however, it is essential to take account of the remaining scene on the cloth Ida and Castore win. In that scene Pallas "di Vulcan vi si vedea vincente" ["is seen victorious over Vulcan"] (*Tes.* 11.61.4). The gloss to this story of the amorous struggle between Vulcan and Minerva is typically lengthy, but its content is unexpected: "Vulcano, iddio del fuoco, chiese a Giove Pallade per moglie. Quella il rifiutò per marito; di che Giove gli concedette che egli, se potesse, prendesse di lei ogni piacere. Di che Vulcano volendola un dì sforzare, fu sì da lei percosso in terra, che egli si guastò l'anca, e sempre poi andò sciancato" ["Vulcan, god of fire, asked Jove for Pallas to be his wife. She refused him as a husband; and for this reason Jove permitted him to take whatever pleasure he could from her. So Vulcan, trying one day to rape her, was so violently knocked to the ground by her that he broke his hip and ever afterwards walked crooked"] (*ad Tes.* 11.61.4).

The common version of this myth ends quite differently: in the excitement of the struggle Vulcan ejaculates, and from his semen Erechthoneus is born, whom Pallas gives to the daughters of Cecrops with instructions that the child be hidden. Turning this episode, which traditionally embarrasses Pallas, into a triumph and associating it with Vulcan's limp is quite unusual. It is also significant because the story in this form is able to play an emblematic role that the more common version certainly could not fulfill.

Boccaccio's historiated cloth tells a consistent story about Pallas, and although the story has Christian significance, the manner of telling it is classical. The allegorical significance of the emblem can be observed in several ways, since the connections between the emblem and the surrounding story are multiple. First and most simply, in his choice of so unusual an object to be historiated there is considerable importance. Arcita is killed by a fall from his horse. It is a response to his manner of death that is suggested first and foremost by this horse trapping. The historiated cloth on the horse responds to the death of the man who fell from a horse. In more general terms, the horse is a conventional symbol of passion in classical and Christian iconography; Pallas is an equally common symbol of wisdom. The historiated cloth representing Pallas, or wisdom, covering the back of the horse, conventionally representing passion, becomes an emblem of the subordination of passion to wisdom. This emblem answers the problem posed by Arcita's death by suggesting that if his *furor* could have been governed in this way, he would not have been destroyed by his mount. In the same way, it serves as a correction of the usurpation by Venus and Mars of the "high hill of Minerva" (*Tes.* 9.2.1).

Theseus has attempted to impose his control over the lovers' passions, however, and he has failed. Either his attempt was not guided by wisdom or the allegory here pertains not to Theseus and the other pagan characters in the poem but only to its Christian readers. Since the vital emblematic details are contained in the lengthy glosses to the poem and are only hinted at in the text itself, I believe that the prizes are interpreted for the readers of the poem in terms eluding the pagan characters. Like Arachne, these characters have a superficial view of what we, with the eyes of Pallas, can see in their fundamental truthfulness.

With the aid of Boccaccio's glosses, the emblems of Pallas can be read in a fully allegorical way. The episodes are these:

1. The sons of Cecrops change their name
2. Minerva invents weaving
3. Minerva invents a musical instrument
4. Minerva defeats Arachne
5. Minerva defeats Vulcan

The first episode records the orientation of the Athenians toward Minerva. To give it an obvious historical significance, it is the birth of the philosophical tradition in Athens; and, in keeping with the suggestion of the passage from Eusebius, it may represent a turn from idolatry.

The significance of this episode, however, as of that of each of the others, is determined by its place in the poem. In a general sense its context is the mourning period that follows the death of Arcita. In terms of its place in the poem, then, this adoption of Athena's name is an adoption of wisdom in the face of death. Of course, death did not come into the world for the first time in the Athens of Theseus. Death entered the world as a consequence of the Fall of Man, and in the same disaster man acquired wisdom. Man uses his wisdom not to change his fallen nature—only Christ will achieve that—but to alleviate the consequences of his Fall, and that is the theme, I believe, of the "onori di Pallade" depicted here.

The first scene is thus the decisive moment when man changes his name and identifies himself with wisdom. The second, Pallas's invention of weaving, is the first art of post-Edenic woman described in Genesis. The third, her invention of a musical instrument, brings solace in the face of pain and labor, themselves primary conditions of fallen man and woman. Arachne is a conventional emblem of pride, a sin often considered the first and most deadly and one that plays a large part in Adam's Fall. He, like her, wished to "aguagliare agl'idii" ["be equal to the gods"]. Wisdom conquers that sin, but it does not destroy it. Finally, Minerva does battle with the "god of fire," who seeks to satisfy his lust by violence in a lewd attempt at *amorosa battaglia*. Wisdom triumphs over both these passions, the violent or irascible and the lustful or concupiscible. It does not destroy their principal, however, as it did not destroy the source of pride, although it cripples him.

There is a sense, too, in this final episode of a more direct conflict between wisdom and death. In describing the burned-out pyre of Arcita, Boccaccio says:

> Il giorno inverso della notte andava,
> e Vulcan lasso in ceneri recate
> le cose avea che ciascun li donava
>
> [The day was turning to night, and a weary Vulcan had reduced to cinders the things that each had given him] (*Tes.* 11.57.1–3).

Boccaccio's "Vulcan lasso" ("weary Vulcan") is a common Latin figure of speech, in which the name of a deity is substituted for that thing with which he is most commonly associated. Boccaccio glosses Vulcan here as "il fuoco" fire (*ad Tes.* 11.57.2), and his expression is modeled directly on Statius's "lassusque . . . Mulciber" (*Theb.* 6.234), in the episode on which this book is based. Nevertheless, it is quite uncommon for Boccaccio to use such a locution, and personification of this sort is seldom seen in his poems. The "weary Vulcan" which had turned all things to ashes is thus a more striking image in *Teseida* than it is in Statius. When, in the space of a few octaves, we see Minerva struggling with this very deity in what appears to be an emblematic contest, it is not unreasonable to see her struggling with the victor over Arcita himself and the victor over all things, death.

This, then, is one reader's understanding of the emblematic "honors of Pallas." They represent wisdom's response not just to the fall of Arcita but to the Fall of Man in general. That response is multiple. The first step is to identify with wisdom and not passion, with the cloth and not the horse. The second is the invention of useful arts, which repair the material damage caused by the Fall. The third is the invention of arts that lighten the human condition and work to redeem human nature. The fourth is the conquest of pride, the fifth, the conquest of passion, and the last, the struggle with death itself, which appropriately crowns a sequence that began in response to one particular death.

One further aspect of this complex emblem remains to be explored: the role that, as it does in its Ovidian precedent, it may play in defining the structure of the poem. Like music, writing can give pleasure, which lightens pain and toil and perhaps softens human nature. If properly understood, in fact, stories contain wisdom and can work the effects that wisdom works, combating passion, pride, and even death. Boccaccio's poem itself is demonstrably like the emblematic honors of Pallas. It figuratively addresses the Fall of Man, just as it literally addresses the fall and death of Arcita. Its aim is to provide a response, even an antidote, to the fundamental human disaster.

As I have already noted, however, the historiated tomb of Arcita, which recapitulates *Teseida* book by book, is a representation of the poem, too. The two artifacts represent the poem in quite different ways, however, and here the cloth of Arachne and that of Pallas, competing representations of the *Metamorphoses*, may be the model. The tomb is literal and may be compared to the weaving of Arachne, which is technically skillful but deficient in content. Like the biblical "letter" which "killeth," it leads to the death of the weaver and here may be appropriately associated with the tomb. The "honors of Pallas," on the other hand, are emblematic and, like the spirit in the word, "give life." The poem as literal history is about death and belongs to the tomb. The poem as emblem is eternally living and life-giving. Against death the emblematic horse trappings set wisdom, the arts to which wisdom gives birth, and the virtues to which wisdom gives aid.

By this juxtaposition, Boccaccio is able to suggest a second response to the reader without disavowing the sequence of the poem either as letter or as history. Boccaccio's Christian reader escapes the literal and historical constraints of the pagan character and finds in the latter's action and world a significance that eludes even the best of the pagans. The emblematic sequence is of fundamental importance in understanding the historical nature of *Teseida*, too, since it is the emblem that allows the poem to maintain its historical integrity and its depiction of a past as past without compromising the poet's need to address his contemporary audience. Through the emblem Boccaccio is able to introduce into his poem a Christian allegorical significance without destroying the historically verisimilar fabric he has labored to create. Rather than destroying history in the poem, the Christian allegory of the honors of Pallas preserves it, since it presents a key to reading history allegorically without equating the two. History remains the province of the characters in the poem; allegory is the province of the reader.

Further allegorical prizes are presented in subsequent games (see Appendix). While they are of great interest in themselves, they preserve the historical and allegorical split apparent in the honors of Pallas and the tomb of Arcita. Even in this brief episode, however, it has been possible to observe Boccaccio's full powers as an imitator of the antique and as an allegorical poet of distinction. As a mimetic artist, he has represented ancient realities in a convincing way through close imitation of Latin epic. As physical objects, his emblems are verisimilar. At the same time, they are Christian allegories, which, if properly perceived, point the way to a metaphorical understanding of crucial issues in the poem. Boccaccio's particular achievement in *Teseida*, then, would seem to be the discovery that, through their differences, history and allegory can reinforce rather than destroy each other. Boccaccio discovers that he can both imitate an epic model and, at the same time, without doing violence to its forms and language, incorporate into it a spur to allegorical understanding. The classical here is by no means merely ornamental, nor can Boccaccio be considered a simple and unsophisticated copier of his epic models. These emblems are both a triumph of imitation and a high point of significance in Boccaccio's poem. That these two should coincide illustrates the thorough interpenetration of meaning and imitation of the antique in *Teseida*.

While the emblems of Pallas present the Christian reader with an allegorical response to Arcita's death, in its final book, *Teseida* presents pagan Athens's response to the same event. All the characters in the poem and Athens in general respond to this death in a way that is appropriate to their historical condition. In a return to the authority that characterized him in the poem's first two books, Theseus guides the community's response. He reasserts the primacy of the gods and the necessity of human subordination, and in the process, he brings about an accommodation of the monuments of the poem to the lives of individual men and women.

In book 12, then, Theseus retreats from his misplaced confidence in individual *pietas* and reasserts man's dependence on the gods and the impropriety as well as the impossibility of opposing them. This necessity, however, need not be joyless, since there are compensations. One of these is fame for the dead; the second compensation is love, but love governed by marriage; and the final monument of the poem encapsulates marriage. In addition, Emilia herself, in a surprising way, is monumentalized. Thus in the end of the poem, too, its monuments continue to symbolize its major themes.

Theseus first responds to the death of Arcita by acknowledging and describing man's necessary subordination to death and to the divine will:

> Così come alcun che mai non visse
> non morì mai, così si pò vedere
> ch'alcun non visse mai che non morisse;
> e noi che ora viviam, quando piacere
> sarà di quel che 'l mondo circunscrisse,
> perciò morremo: adunque sostenere
> il piacer dell'iddii lieti dobbiamo,
> poi ch'ad esso resister non possiamo
>
> [Just as one who never lived never yet
> died, so one can see that no one ever

lived yet who has not died; and we who
live now, when it is the pleasure of him
who circumscribed the globe, we, too,
will die: and therefore we must endure
the pleasure of the gods with joy since
we cannot resist them] (*Tes.* 12.6).

Theseus counsels that they make virtue of this necessity:

E però far della necessitate
virtù, quando bisogna, è sapienza,
e il contrario è chiara vanitate

[And therefore to make
virtue of necessity, when
there is need, is wisdom; and
the opposite is plain foolish-
ness] (*Tes.* 12.11.1–3).

Therefore, Theseus argues, even in Arcita's early death there is good:

E certo io credo ch'allora migliore
la morte sia quando di viver giova;
il modo e dove l'uom che ha valore
nol de' curar, ché dovunque el si trova,
fama li serba il suo debito onore

[And I certainly believe that death is
better when one is still enjoying life.
How it happens and where, the man
of courage need care nothing about;
for wherever he is Fame will give him
his due honor] (*Tes.* 12.9.1–5).

Theseus dwells at length on the idea of fame. He recommends the example of Arcita, who

fu tanto e tal, che grazioso frutto
di fama s'ha lasciato dietro al fiore

[was such that he left the gracious
fruit of fame after his flowering]
(*Tes.* 12.12.3–4).[27]

If we consider the meaning and course of his life, Theseus concludes,

> se ben pensassomo, al postutto
> lasciar dovremmo il misero dolore,
> e intender a vita valorosa
> che ci acquistasse fama gloriosa
>
> [if we have well considered after all, we should give up our miserable sadness and concentrate on the life of valor which can win us glorious fame] (*Tes.* 12.12.5–8).

This, then, is Theseus's first consolation for the death of Arcita; he has acquired fame through his valor, and his life serves as an example and a spur to acquire fame. There are two medieval traditions of fame.[28] One fame is worldly and fickle, and, like other goods of fortune, with which it is linked, it is unreliable in its report and unfair in its object. The other is a Christian tradition in which fame takes part in the glory of God himself.

Theseus's speeches about fame serve as verbal capstones to the monumental structure of the poem, particularly as those monuments have come to reflect the tragic loss of Arcita. What Theseus says, in fact, is represented on the historiated tomb of Arcita, described at the end of book 11. That monument, in effect, contains the fame of Arcita. In Theseus's speech, moreover, the notion of fame becomes a dominating force in the structure of the poem as a whole and in the view of paganism it offers. The poem, having organized and defined itself in terms of temples, theaters, and tombs, represents the ancient world as constructed or subsumed by monuments. Theseus's discourse has the effect of placing those monuments within the tradition of fame.

Monuments such as Arcita's tomb, however, reflect the tradition of worldly fame. There Arcita's story is fixed, and it represents "the importance of worldly renown as an object of idolatrous worship."[29] Such idolatry is well suited to a pagan temple, and the fact that such fame is strictly limited in time, as Petrarch portrays it in *Trionfi*, makes the argument more convincing.[30] The stone temple subject to time's destruction and dedicated to the cult of the dead seems an excellent symbol of just this limited kind of earthly fame.

The historiated prizes offered at his funeral games respond in a different way to Theseus's discussion of fame. They do not enshrine Arcita's story as the temple-tomb does; instead, they respond to Arcita's life and death by showing how in response to it the champions of Greece cultivated "la vita valorosa" ("the valorous life") that Theseus urges. Fame that depends on virtue's response to a virtuous life is more in keeping with the other face of the medieval tradition of fame. When fame is "sought for its own sake, it leads to idolatry, a glorification of God's gifts as objects of worship. When based upon charity and good works, it is a means of glorifying God and achieving salvation."[31]

While it is not by any means "charity and good works" that the funeral games embody, the games do show martial virtues in action. They produce for their pagan participants an enduring kind of fame. The emblematic prizes in these games, however, directly enshrine and celebrate the Christian virtues on which this second kind of fame depends.

Theseus's final speech to his mourning court again addresses the monumental structure of the poem. It does not do so in precisely thematic terms; he does not recapitulate the significant monuments. He does, however, address monumentality itself. He suggests that

> [il] corpo che riman, nulla altra prova
> fa in un loco che in altro morto,
> né l'alma n'ha più pena e men diporto
>
> [the body which remains has no
> worse suffering lying dead in one
> place than in another; nor does the
> soul have more pain or less pleasure]
> (*Tes.* 12.9.6–8).

The tomb is of little consequence, then, and by implication the kind of fame that goes with the tomb is of equally little importance. The fame that inspires virtue and is reflected in valorous acts is the only thing that matters.

This dichotomy suggests yet another response to the monumentality of the poem as a whole. After all, Arcita's monument is by no means the only structure in the poem, as I have repeatedly observed. The wealth of temples and the majestic theater occupy and define much of *Teseida*. These structures and the actions they contain and imply partake to some extent of the condemnation of Arcita's tomb. Depending on the response of virtue, a temple of Venus may be the scene of divinely inspired reconciliation, as it is in Scythia. If virtue is absent or overridden by other forces, a temple of the same goddess (this time in Athens) can make possible a triumph of fury and death. As virtue springs from them or is seconded by them, these monuments in the poem suggest one sort of fame or another.

The poet's role is also embraced by the concept of fame, for it is he who assigns, preserves, or resuscitates it. He distinguishes fame from infamy and eternal from temporal glory. Inevitably, his action leads to a process of reading the past that either reinvests the monumental with significance or strips it of pretension. Where virtue is present, the poet gives life and eternal fame. Where it is absent, the poet leaves the ancient world substantially as he finds it, a field of scattered monuments linked to death.

Two other monuments remain in the poem, the temple of Venus in which the wedding of Emilia and Palemone is finally celebrated as well as a much more surprising structure. The existence of this second "structure" is implied by the language Boccaccio uses in an invocation to the Muses:

> O sante donne, le quali Anfione
> ataste a chiuder Tebe, or fa mestiere
> che da voi sia atato il mio sermone
> acciò ch' io possa dimostrar le vere
> bellezze che mostrò 'n quella stagione Emilia

> [O holy ladies, who helped Amphion to enclose Thebes, now make it your business to help me, so that I can show the true beauties that Emilia displayed at that time] (*Tes.* 12.52.1–5).

Boccaccio asks aid in describing Emilia from the Muses, who helped the mythical poet Amphion to build the walls of Thebes. The implication is that Emilia and Thebes are similar structures. Such a notion, while it seems more than a little odd, may serve as a metaphor of the way that fiction invests monumentality with life. Thebes, the dead structure, is given life in the woman Emilia. Her geographical-sounding name, like that of Lavinia, has already suggested such a fusion of person and place, if not person and thing.

Her husband's succession to the throne of his kingdom is conventionally seen in terms of marriage as well. What is most significantly symbolized by this fusion, however, is a marriage by which the sensuality focused around Emilia will be given expression through marriage. That sensuality is especially important as the last survival of her Scythian past as well as Arcita's Theban one.

The wedding takes place in the great temple of Venus (*Tes.* 12.67.2). This goddess was last seen as the sponsor of a murderous Fury, and though it might appear that one Venus has again substituted for another, this is not the case. When Palemone invoked the aid of Venus (*Tes.* 7.43–49), he was furious, and the aid he received came in the form of fury. Here he invokes the goddess again in the multiple reconciliations of marriage. His fury is no longer raging, and he can receive the goddess differently. So in the last book, as in the first, she emerges as the force presiding over the union of man and woman. She is accompanied here by Hymen, the legitimating force of marriage.

This wedding implies a number of reconciliations in the poem. Venus's champion, Palemone, weds Diana's virgin Amazon. Thebes and Scythia, the impious and cruel nations Theseus battled, are finally joined in marriage under his supervision and under the protection of the gods. In this temple, at last, one can speak of the *pietas* of Theseus as finally triumphant, as it collaborates with the gods and the *furor* of his opponents.

The principal reconciliation involves the goddess Juno, who also attends. Throughout the poem she has acted as the jealous deity who punishes the grandsons of Cadmus. Here, however, her aid is invoked as the goddess of marriage (*Tes.* 12.68.8). This final role recalls the double part she plays in *Filocolo,* where she is both the instigator of change through violent means and the pacifier through marriage. The presence of Venus and Juno at this wedding suggests the reconciliation of these goddesses with each other, with Jupiter, and with fate, which occurs near the end of the *Aeneid* and which prepares for the final reconciliation of Trojans and Latins and the end of the fratricidal war in Italy.

Marriage represents the final reconciliation of *pietas* and *furor. Furor,* no longer threatening but joyous, has its final reflection in *Teseida* when Palemone and Emilia finally meet as lovers. Then the fires of love, which destroyed Arcita and the lovely bosk, reappear in manageable although apparently stimulating form:

> Vero è che per l'offerte che andaro
> poi la mattina a' templi, s'argomenta
> che Venere, anzi che 'l dì fosse chiaro,
> sette volte raccesa e tante spenta
> fosse nel fonte amoroso
>
> [From the offerings that went to the temple the morning after, truly it would seem that Venus, before the day was light, was seven times rekindled and as many quenched in the font of love] (*Tes.* 12.77.1–5).

It is likely that such activity will still the *furor* of Theban and Scythian and that marriage under Theseus's sovereignty will be an image of the marriage of reason and sensuality. In this way apparently, but only in this way, can Theseus conquer *furor* with *pietas*.

Teseida, then, is a complex achievement for Boccaccio. It caps a sequence of works in which classical culture is imitated extensively and examined critically. *Filostrato,* the first work in the sequence, is the story of those who, unlike Aeneas, do not outlive Troy's fall. In the implied contrast between Troilus and Aeneas, it shows the crucial differences between a survivor and a man doomed to share Troy's destruction. Troilus gives himself up to passion and *furor* and, as a result, finds death in a war that Aeneas, with divine aid, survives. In effect, *Filostrato* differentiates Troilus and Aeneas in moral terms and, more significantly, in terms of responsiveness to divine intervention. *Filocolo,* too, engages themes of the *Aeneid.* However, it concentrates more on the providential than on the tropological. From its beginning, the romance is concerned with the action of divinity in history, with the conversion of nations, and with their falling away from faith. In this romance an Orosian reading of Roman history is laid over the fated and divinely appointed mission of Aeneas. That reading is then extended to include periods of history after Orosius's day in which a similar providential pattern is seen.

Teseida in some sense combines the themes of the earlier texts, but just as *Filocolo* differs from *Filostrato* in its presentation of human passions and failings, *Teseida* differs from *Filocolo* in its view of the divine. In *Teseida* there is no constant collaboration between human and divine will. Theseus's *pietas* seeks response from gods who represent themselves, in a critical phase of the romance, as demonic. Men dominated by *furor* find in these gods a willingness to respond in kind, and the result is disaster. The theme of *Teseida,* then, is the limits of human action and human potential unaided by grace. *Teseida* shows how little man in opposition to divinity can do to impose order on himself and society. Individual *pietas* cannot control *furor,* and in the wake of failure *Teseida* explores wisdom, fame, the consolations of humility, and finally the joy of another kind of *furor,* love expressed in marriage. This increasing complexity of theme suggests a growing engagement with the antique and an increasing sophistication in coming to terms with the argument of Vergil's epic. To move from general questions of passion and wrath, to historical questions carried from legendary times to the century before Boccaccio's own, to problems that express themselves in words borrowed from the *Aeneid* itself, is a long series of steps. Theseus's continual portrayal in terms of *pietas* is a significant engagement of Vergil's central theme. The continual and systematic references to Aeneas, Turnus, Lavinia, Mezentius, and Dido are equal evidence of the poem's close engagement of this model.

This rather long story has brought us to this ending. Quite unexpectedly, Boccaccio, a neophyte poet living in Naples, beyond the pale of Tuscan or northern Italian culture, in the 1330s created a series of classicizing romances that show extraordinary understanding of the material culture of the ancient world and of the major themes of its greatest poetry. He presents the ancient world as past and separated from the present by its paganism. He simultaneously presents it as timeless and engaged in man's continual struggle with his own passions. It is a world caught between *pietas* and *furor,* between providential history and universal damnation. His poems serve, too, as a series of complex meditations on the *Aeneid,* where the love of Dido and Aeneas, the mission of Aeneas to found Rome, and the divinely sanctioned task of Romanization are repeatedly examined. These romances form an extraordinarily vital, historically significant, and continually rewarding group of texts that serve in many senses as the cornerstones of Renaissance archaeology and Renaissance allegorical epic and romance.

Appendix

Prizes in the Funeral Games of Arcita

THE HISTORIATED PRIZE IN honor of Pallas, which I have considered at great length, is only one of the prizes presented in the games in book 11 of *Teseida.* It is, however, the most complex and the most significant, and the other prizes, which are also emblematic, reinforce themes suggested by that one. Not only are the prizes similar in each game, but, as in the case of the footrace, only the prize, and not the contest, is described in detail. The effect of this is to make the funeral games a series of emblems in the manner of an allegorical pageant. In this way Boccaccio not only imitates the epic practice of including funeral games but also turns them to integral use in the structure of his poem. Vergil's funeral games of Anchises and Statius's games for Opheltes are not merely ornamental. Neither are those of Boccaccio. Each has a role to play in the economy of the poem as a whole. Nor is Boccaccio's the least successful adaptation of this convention to the purposes of his own creation.

Following the footrace is a wrestling match, in which Theseus himself participates and which indeed he wins:

> Ma poi nell'unta palestra Teseo
> per virtù propria meritò l'onore,
> però ch'al tempo suo me' ch'altro il feo,
> e ben lo seppe Elena
>
> [But then in the oiled wrestling Theseus,
> because of his own skill, deserved the
> honors, since in his time he did it better
> than any other, as Helen well knew]
> (*Tes.* 11.62.1–4).

Theseus's skill in the palaestra and the nature of that game are explained in earlier glosses to the poem to which the glosses at this point refer.[1] Through the use of the word "palaestra" and these references to early glosses, Boccaccio links the game and ultimately the prize associated with it to a significant earlier moment in the text. Before the contest in the theater, which leads to Arcita's death, Theseus expresses surprise at the champions each Theban hero has brought to be his seconds:

> Ma, certo quand' io loro in pace posi
> e nelle man di cento e cento diedi
> l'amor di quella ond'eran sì bramosi,
> non mi credetti che lance né spiedi
> né troppi ferri chiari o rugginosi
> né gran cavai né grandi uomini a piedi
> dovesser terminar cotanto foco,
> ma esser ciò com'un palestral gioco
>
> [But certainly when I made peace between them, and gave into the hands of two companies of a hundred the love of her of whom they are so desirous, I did not believe that lances and spears nor too many shining or rusty swords nor great horses nor great foot soldiers should bring such a fire to its end, but that this would be like a palaestral game] (*Tes.* 7.4).

Just as the reference in Arcita's funeral games leads us back to this first significant mention of the palaestral game, this paragraph looks forward, not to those games, but to the fire itself. It is not, as Theseus imagines, for so much steel and muscle to terminate the fire of love, but the funeral pyre prevails and consumes with it fifteen of the champions here and a considerable share of dedicated spears, lances, and swords. These forward and backward reflecting ironies show the degree to which the contest in the theater has continually eluded Theseus's control.

Boccaccio understands the nature of the palaestra well enough, although he makes one very curious mistake.[2] Palaestra was a form of wrestling, as he says; both men and women competed in it, and they did anoint their skins with at least oil, if not tallow, before taking part in it. They competed naked, however, and the skins they anointed were their own. Boccaccio describes such wrestlers as wearing a formfitting leather garment. This has no ancient precedent. It may have been invented by his source, or he himself may have added it to accommodate the imagination to Helen's participation in the sport.

This sensual aspect of the sport makes it a good image for the *amorosa battaglia* that Theseus intends for the lovers in the theater. When the palaestra is reintroduced in celebration of Arcita's funeral, this amorous aspect is still present, and Helen is again recalled and Theseus's skill reaffirmed (*Tes.* 11.62.4). Theseus's prize, however, is a shield recording triumphs of Apollo:

> nel qual vedeasi Marsia sonando,
> sé con Appollo nel sonar provando.
> Vedeasi appresso superar Fitone,
> e quindi sotto l'ombre graziose,
> sopra Parnaso, presso a l'Elicone
> fonte seder con le nove amorose
> Muse e cantar maestrevol canzone;
> e oltre a queste v'eran molte cose,
> tutte in onor di Febo
>
> [on which was seen Marsyas playing and competing with Apollo at playing. Nearby [Apollo] was seen overcoming the Pythian serpent, and then in comfortable shade on Parnassus, near the fount of Helicon seated with the nine amorous Muses and singing a masterful song; and in addition to these there were many things all in honor of Phoebus] (*Tes.* 11.62.6–63.7).

In many ways this prize resembles that offered for the footrace. It is a historiated shield, not a horse cloth, and as such it is a common motif of epic poetry, based on the shield of Aeneas described in *Aeneid* 8.608–731.[3] The dedicatee and the subject recall that of the earlier historiated prize. Apollo and Pallas have similar ties to the intellect and to philosophy; the episodes depicted bear some resemblances. Apollo defeats Marsyas in a contest, just as Minerva defeats Arachne. Apollo overcomes a man-threatening serpent, just as Minerva overcomes Neptune, not himself a monster but a god who in this episode overwhelms and drowns men with a monstrous lake.

Whereas in the story of Minerva the arts were emphasized, however, here in Apollo's story art itself is featured. Nevertheless, there is no great difference between the role art plays in the two emblems. The art of music, already alluded to in Minerva's invention of the flute, is here given a more generous treatment. The role that music plays in the life of man and the role that song plays are not to be understood differently here from the way they are presented in the honors of Pallas. The connections between the palaestral game as Boccaccio describes it here and the triumphs of Apollo are ironic. Reference to the palaestra recalls Theseus's failure to regulate the contest in the theater, and this suggests that the Apollonian shield (like the emblem of Minerva) is a response to that earlier sequence of events. Devotion to the amorous Muses is a substitute or compensation for devotion to the "amorosa battaglia" of the oily palaestra.

The next game described is the form of Greek and Roman boxing called *caestus*. Boccaccio is uncertain about the nature of the game, as he himself admits.[4] As in the other two games, the prize is more important than the game. Here it is two large cups:

> In essi con non poca sottigliezza
> era scolpito Alcide nella cuna
> ancor giacente prender con fierezza
> le serpi a lui mandate e ad ognuna
> la morte dare; e quindi la fortezza
> ch'egli usò nella nemea selva bruna
> contra 'l fiero leone, e quindi appresso
> l'altre fatiche sue v'eran con esso
>
> [In these [Hercules] was sculpted with no little subtlety; still lying in his cradle, he takes the serpents sent to him with pride and kills them both; then is shown the force he used in the dark Nemean wilderness against the proud lion, and there besides the other labors were depicted with these] (*Tes.* 11.65).

Like Apollo, Hercules is a monster slayer, but unlike Apollo or Minerva, he has no other emblematic role to play. Boccaccio's glosses briefly explain the two scenes depicted: "Eran in questi nappi intagliate le XII fatiche d'Alcide, cioè d'Ercule; delle quali qui di due solamente fa menzione. La prima è che essendo egli ancora picciolo fanciullo nella culla, Giunone, sua matrigna, mandò due serpi ad ucciderlo, le quali due serpi Ercule, così piccolo come era, prese e uccise. La seconda si è del leone, il quale egli nella selva chiamata Nemea ucccise" ["On these cups the twelve labors of Alcides, that is, Hercules, were inscribed; of which only two are mentioned here. The first is this: while he was still a little baby in his crib, Juno, his stepmother, sent two serpents to kill him, which Hercules, as little as he was, took and killed. The second is of the lion which he killed in the wilderness called Nemea"] (*ad Tes.* 11.65.1).

Hercules can properly stand as an emblem of self-control, the physical attribute that complements wisdom, but this emblem, like the other two, has a direct reference to events in the poem. This is implicit in both labors described. In the first, Juno's antipathy toward Hercules and his response are shown, and that response contrasts strongly with the reply that the Theban knights make to the same opposition. Arcita recalls the violent interference of Juno in Theban affairs when he laments:

> Omè, che m'era assai maravigliosa
> cosa a pensar che Iunon ci lasciasse
> nostra vita menare in tanta posa,
> e come i nostri noi non stimolasse
>
> [Oh, it was a marvelous thing for
> me to think that Juno would let
> us lead our lives in such repose,
> and not goad us as she did our
> ancestors] (*Tes.* 5.56.1–4).

It is this goading on to violence that Hercules would seem, ironically, to overcome in conquering the serpents sent by Juno. The Theban knights are unable to resist it.

The second labor recalls the battle in the theater where, even though they have been removed from the wilderness, their passion likens them, as Boccaccio's similes show, to wild beasts. It is Arcita himself who is compared to the lion (*Tes.* 7.115). Hercules triumphs over "il fiero leone," but Arcita is the lion, and it is this bestial aspect of himself, which Hercules conquers, that destroys Arcita. Just as Troilus is compared to a libidinous Hercules, here Arcita is contrasted with a heroic Hercules.[5]

The last game held is the discus.[6] The prize in this contest is the simplest of all—a helmet—

> e 'n forma di pastore
> su vi sedeva Pan iddio sonando,
> in quella vera forma che gli danno
> gli Arcadi allor che figurar lo fanno.

> [and on it in the form of a shepherd
> the god Pan was seated, playing,
> in that true form that the Arcadi-
> ans give him when they have him
> depicted] (*Tes.* 11.66.5–8).

Unfortunately, this interesting object is accompanied by an incomplete gloss. We cannot know what Boccaccio thought the "true form" of Arcadian Pan might be. Pan's meaning, however, can be guessed at on the basis of the other emblems. He combines the musical traits of Apollo and Minerva and is also associated with the woods in a way that might relate him to Hercules. In texts that Boccaccio knows well and to which he turns again and again, Vergil and Ovid, Pan plays a part that can be related to the other emblems in this collection. In the *Metamorphoses,* Ovid tells the story of Pan and Syrinx (*Met.* 1.689–712). The god sees, desires, and speaks to a beautiful nymph, a follower of Diana. She refuses to hear him and runs away, but a lake prevents her escape. On its borders she prays to her sister nymphs of the water. They hear her and transform her into a reed. When Pan reaches for her, his hand grasps a reed. The wind blowing in it produces a pleasant sound, and so he gathers several reeds of different lengths and makes music on them.

> Arte nova vocisque deum dulcedine captum
> "hoc mihi conloquium tecum" dixisse "manebit"

> [The god, captivated by the new art and the
> sweetness of its voice, said, "This talk with you
> will remain with me"] (*Met.* 1.709–10).

The song as a substitute for the conversation Syrinx denies Pan seems similar to the choice of the amorous Muses in preference to *amorosa battaglia.* Pan also plays a similar role in Vergil's *Eclogues.* He is one of several gods who discourage the impassioned Gallus in his intentions.

Pan deus Arcadiae venit, quem vidimus ipsi
sanguineis ebuli bacis minioque rubentem.
"ecquis erit modus?" inquit. "Amor non talia curat
nec lacrimis crudelis Amor nec gramina rivis
nec cutiso saturantur apes nec fronde capellae"

[Pan the god of Arcadia came, whom we saw ourselves ruddy with the blood-colored berries of the dwarf-elder and with cinnabar. "Is there no limit?" he asks. "Love has no mind for such things; nor by tears is cruel love, nor by streams meadows, nor are bees sated with shrub-trefoil nor she-goats by a leafy branch"][7]

Pan's plea here seems to be that there is no temperance in such love and that it is in the nature of cruel love to be so immoderate. If we take this to be Pan's song to Syrinx, it is easy to see Pan as one who, in the manner of Hercules, exerts self-control and one who, in the manner of Apollo or Minerva, helps others through his singing to attain the same control. Pan is another for whom song substitutes for other kinds of action. He emerges, then, as a fitting culmination of the series of emblems that begins with Minerva, for he possesses a kind of self-control communicated through singing, the very model of the allegorical poet, whose song, as Hamlet says of the skillful actor, "begets a temperance."[8]

The games, then, are exceptionally important; they represent an unprecedented attempt to include ancient contests in a medieval poem. The games are described in glosses, as I have shown, and the poem concentrates on the prizes awarded. The prizes—horses, embroidered cloths, a pair of cups, a decorated shield, a historiated helmet—all have epic precedents. They are appropriate objects to be awarded at the kinds of games Boccaccio describes. Their role in the poem, however, as I have emphasized, transcends the physical and the historical. The prizes are emblematic, and the emblems have a larger role to play. That role is governed by the position of the games as part of the funeral of Arcita. The emblems of the games respond to the death, both in specific and in general terms. Each emblem recalls a significant event in the history of Arcita and proposes a corrective. In broad terms the emblems respond to the fallen or pagan condition of man. They emphasize the physical, emotional, and spiritual arts—with prominence placed on music—that enable man to respond to the Fall and to its concomitant, death.

Notes

Preface

1 D. S. Brewer, "The Relationship of Chaucer to the English and European Traditions," in *Chaucer and Chaucerians,* ed. D. S. Brewer (London: Macmillan, 1966), 1–38; Nicholas R. Havely, *Chaucer's Boccaccio* (Woodbridge, U.K.: D. S. Brewer; Totowa, NJ: Rowman and Littlefield, 1980); Piero Boitani, *Chaucer and Boccaccio,* Medium Aevum Monographs, n.s. 8 (Oxford: Society for the Study of Mediaeval Languages and Literature, 1977); Piero Boitani, *Chaucer and the Italian Trecento* (Cambridge: Cambridge University Press, 1983); David Wallace, *Chaucer and the Early Writings of Boccaccio* (Woodbridge, U.K.: D. S. Brewer, 1985). See also David Anderson, *Before the Knight's Tale* (Philadelphia: University of Pennsylvania Press, 1988). While Anderson's book appeared before mine, my extensive article on the *Teseida* in *Modern Language Notes,* which raises many of the points I amplify here, is quoted by Anderson ("Boccaccio's Athenian Theater: Form and Function of an Ancient Monument in *Teseida, MLN* 99 [1984]: 1–42).

1 Introduction

1 James H. McGregor, *The Image of Antiquity in Boccaccio's "Filostrato," "Filocolo," and "Teseida,"* vol. 1 of *Studies in Italian Culture: Literature and History,* ed. Aldo Scaglione (New York: Peter Lang, 1990). See also McGregor, "Boccaccio's Athenian Theater."

2 Vittore Branca, the dean of Boccaccio critics, has expressed this view repeatedly; see below, chap. 2, n. 4.

3 The standard biography of Boccaccio is Vittore Branca, *Giovanni Boccaccio: Profilo biografico* (Florence: Sansoni, 1977). Much of this material is available in English in Branca, *Boccaccio: The Man and His Works,* trans. Richard Monges (New York: Harvester Press, 1976), and Judith Powers Serafini-Sauli, *Giovanni Boccaccio,* Twayne World Authors Series 644 (Boston: Twayne, 1982).

4 For the standard view of the limitations of Boccaccio's Neapolitan experience, see Giorgio Padoan, *Il Boccaccio, Le Muse, il Parnaso, e l'Arno* (Florence: Olschki, 1978), 3–12.

5 MS Florence, National Library, B.R. 50.

6 MS Florence, Laurentian Library, Plut. 29, 8.

7 Guy Raynaud de Lage, "Les Romans antiques et la representation de l'antiquité," *Moyen Age* 67 (1960): 247–91. See also Jean Frappier, "Remarques sur la peinture de la vie et des héros antiques dans la littérature française du XIIe et du XIIIe siècle," in *L'Humanisme médiévale dans les littératures romanes du XIIe et du XIIIe siècle (Colloque de Strasbourg)* (Paris: Klincksieck, 1964): 13–54; Omer Jodogne, "Le Caractère des oeuvres 'antiques' dans la littérature française du XIIe et du XIIIe siècle," in *L'Humanisme médiévale,* ibid., 55–85; Renate Blumenfeld-Kosinski, "Old French Narrative Genres: Towards the Definition of the Roman Antique," *Romance Philology* 34 (1980): 143–59.

8 For this negative assessment, see Roberto Weiss, *The Renaissance Discovery of Classical Antiquity* (Oxford: Blackwell's, 1969), 30–31.

9 Robert Hanning, *The Vision of History in Early Britain* (New York: Columbia University Press, 1966), 39.

10 Ibid., 38.

11 See, especially, *Inferno* 2.13–24, where Aeneas's mission is made to culminate in the foundation of that city, "u' siede il successor del maggior Piero" (*Inf.* 2.24). In *Paradiso* 6, Justinian explains the history of early Christianity in terms that reflect the *Aeneid* and Orosius.

12 Robert Hollander, *Il Virgilio dantesco: Tragedia nella "Commedia," Biblioteca di "Lettere Italiane,"* Studi e Testi, no. 28 (Florence: Olschki, 1983).

13 Paul Renucci, *Dante: Disciple et juge du monde greco-latin* (Paris: Les Belles Lettres, 1954).

14 "E nondimeno vero che Virgilio viene condannato nella sua opera come pagano" (Hollander, *Virgilio dantesco,* 148).

15 Charles G. Osgood, ed. and trans., *Boccaccio on Poetry* (Englewood Cliffs, NJ: Prentice-Hall, 1967), 68; Boccaccio, *Genealogie deorum* 14.13.

16 Branca dates the *Filostrato* "1335?" (*Profilo,* 41). See also P. G. Ricci, "Per la datazione del *Filostrato,*" *Studi sul Boccaccio* 1 (1963): 333–48. Dating is discussed in Vittore Branca's introduction to his edition of *Filostrato* (hereafter cited parenthetically as *Filos.*) in vol. 2 of *Tutte le opere di Giovanni Boccaccio,* ed. Vittore Branca (Milan: Mondadori, 1964). The Mondadori edition, projected in twelve volumes, of which six have appeared, is the standard edition of all the works of Boccaccio I am discussing, and all citations of Boccaccio's works here are to that edition. This and all subsequent translations are mine.

17 Branca dates *Filocolo* "1336–38?" (*Profilo,* 44). Antonio Enzo Quaglio, in his edition of *Filocolo* (hereafter cited parenthetically as *Filoc.*), in vol. 1 of *Tutte le opere di Giovanni Boccaccio,* ed. Vittore Branca (Milan: Mondadori, 1967), 47, concurs.

18 Branca dates *Teseida* "1339–41" (*Profilo,* 49). Alberto Limentani, in his edition of *Teseida* (hereafter cited parenthetically as *Tes.*) in vol. 2 of *Tutte le opere di Giovanni Boccaccio,* ed. Vittore Branca (Milan: Mondadori, 1964), 231, agrees.

2 *Filostrato*

1 *Filostrato,* proemio, par. 25–26, defines the narrator's method for expressing his "doglia nel petto nascosa. . . . E il modo fu questo: di dovere in persona d'alcuno passionato, sì come io ero e sono, cantando narrare li miei martiri." If the narrator here and Boccaccio are assumed to be one and the same, autobiographical criticism of the poem is seemingly encouraged by the text itself. For the difference between Boccaccio and his narrative personae, see Robert Hollander, *Boccaccio's Two Venuses* (New York: Columbia University Press, 1977), 92–116.

2 This assumption had importance for the dating of the poem itself. As Vittore Branca summarizes, "In questo romanzesco quadro, la composizione del *Filostrato* fu fatta risalire dal Crescini (1887) a un periodo anteriore alle intime relazioni del poeta con la sua amata; si convenne anzi di porla attorno al 1336. La data fu in generale accettata dalla critica; fino allo studio del Pernicone (1929) che, con analoga metodologia, sostenne che il *Filostrato* era stato scritto 'in un periodo di tempo in cui il Boccaccio tutto aveva ottenuto dalla sua Fiammetta,' cioè verso il 1338" (*Filos.* 3). Branca dates the poem by a similar method, which reveals his transformation of the "autobiographical" into self-conscious myth creation. *Filostrato,* he argues, "appare . . . anteriore al definirsi del mito letterario di Fiammetta" (4). By this transfiguration, Branca has evaded some but not all of the pitfalls of autobiographical criticism.

3 Branca sees Boccaccio's own amorous experience as animating his French sources: "L'episodio, anticipato contenutisticamente dal romanzo francese, è illuminato da un interesse sentimentale del tutto nuovo attraverso l'approfondimento psicologico di un'esperienza d'amore che nello scrittore doveva essere appassionata e immediata (autobiografica in senso lato)" (ibid., 7).

4 In the preface to his edition, Branca considers the text in terms of three elements: in terms of the sources of the narrative in French, Latin, and both learned and popular Italian literature; in terms of Boccaccio's own experience of love; and in terms of his development as an artist. He does not even refer to the interpretation of the text. Padoan refers to the traditional assessment of the cultural atmosphere of the Angevin court and to Boccaccio's acquisition of "la tematica della grande forza dell'Amore che vince ognuno ed ogni cosa, nel cui nome si infrangano anche le leggi del matrimonio e le fanciulle si oppongono alla clausura in convento. . . . Inoltre già nelle prime rime appare il tema . . . della 'saviezza': la saviezza del saper cogliere l'occasione fortunata, del superare il timore pudico di fanciulla" (*Boccaccio: Le Muse,* 12–13). This concentration on "saviezza" links *Filostrato* with the worldliness critics have often found expressed in the *Decameron.* Many critics, Padoan among them, have seen the *opere minori* as of interest primarily as steps toward the development of Boccaccio's mature art.

5 Branca says, "Nell'atmosfera che trasforma la mitica Troia in una 'città grande e dilettosa' che 'in tregua' svolge una vita tranquilla e operosa, da grande comune medievale, si inquadrano coerentemente scene di vita tipicamente borghese" (*Filos.,* 12). Serafini-Sauli observes, "Neither paganism nor Christianity forms the ideological substratum and the classical elements

are at most ornamental. Though based on a pagan story, the *Filostrato* is turned into a story about love for pleasure, or lust in conformity with medieval courtly canons" (*Giovanni Boccaccio,* 29). Vittore Branca states, "Those warriors—they may be called Troilus or Diomedes, Pandarus or Ulysses, Hector or Achilles—are not mythical heroes but knights of the court, people belonging not to epic but romance" ("The Myth of the Hero in Boccaccio," in *Concepts of the Hero in the Middle Ages,* Fourth and Fifth Annual Conferences of the Center for Medieval and Early Renaissance Studies, ed. Norman T. Burns and C. J. Reagen [Albany: State University of New York Press, 1975], 269).

6 It is more common to see the initial scenes of the poem, with their Trojan emphases, as giving way to unrelated amorous materials. Hollander argues, "The narrative portion of the *Filostrato* begins and ends in epic dress. . . . In between these two military scenes there is precious little that deals with arms" (*Boccaccio's Two Venuses,* 49).

7 This scene is a "Begegnung im Tempel," a scene of falling in love in a temple, which is patterned on the first meeting of Dido and Aeneas. See Bernhard König, *Die Begegnung im Tempel: Abwandlungen eines literarischen Motivs in den Werken Boccaccios* (Hamburg: De Gruyter, 1960). See my *Image of Antiquity,* chap. 1, for a lengthy recapitulation of König's argument.

8 See R. G. Austin, ed., *Vergili Maronis Aeneidos liber secundus* (Oxford: Clarendon Press, 1964), 83–85 n. 163.

9 Antenor, for whom Criseida is exchanged, does not die at Troy: he escapes and founds Padua (see *Aeneid* [*Aen.*] 1.242–49). That she is traded for a survivor perhaps exemplifies the choice that love for her implies between death at Troy and life elsewhere. In the majority of texts collected by Maria Gozzi, "Sulle fonti del *Filostrato,*" *Studi sul Boccaccio* 5 (1958): 123–209, Antenor is the only Trojan captive mentioned. He is exchanged not for Criseida but for the Greek Thoas.

10 Diomedes, who "steals" Criseida from Troilus, shares in the theft of the Palladium as well. The sources described by Maria Gozzi in "Sulle fonti del *Filostrato*" 168–77, do not show Diomedes using the course of the war as his argument. His seduction in those accounts is not especially suited to the situation of the war. In the *Historia destructionis Troiae,* for example, "Sui ardoris flammam continere non valens Briseide revelat sui estuantis cordis amorem, quam in multis affectuosis sermonibus et blandiciis necnon promissionibus revera magnificis allicere satis humiliter est conatus." The difference of their nations is dismissed in other texts by a proverb, as in the *Libro della storia di Troia:* "Io credo che voi amarete tutti giorni quelli della città, perciò che nudrita v'hanno . . . ma io ho udito sovente parlare che genti che non s'avranno mai vedute né conoscuite, si so' amate insieme" (Gozzi, "Sulle fonti del *Filostrato,*" 168, 175).

11 Gozzi, ibid., offers no parallels for this significant scene. Deiphobus here, in effect, gives Troilus his death blow. According to the *Aeneid,* he marries Helen after Paris's death and is betrayed by her. Aeneas talks with his horribly mutilated shade in *Aeneid* 6.494–547. R. D. Williams, in *Aeneid of Vergil,* 2 vols. (London: Macmillan, 1972–73), notes that "Deiphobus' fate exemplifies the fate of all those comrades of Aeneas who did not survive the

sack of Troy" (1:490 n. 494). (All *Aeneid* quotes are from this edition; the *Aeneid* translations are mine.) Deiphobus, then, the victim of Helen and of the choices she represents, is a fitting instrument of Troilus's destruction.

12 Hollander argues that "the praise of love which we find in the *Filostrato* should probably be understood as being the praise offered by fools and knaves" (*Boccaccio's Two Venuses,* 50). He argues, too, that "Troilus was right, if callow, at the beginning, when he thought himself well out of the chains of love; when he was free. That word . . . is perhaps the key word in Boccaccio's negative view of carnal love, which robs us of that precious freedom of choice that makes the next world possible and this world livable" (52). Robert ap Roberts, in "Love in the *Filostrato,*" *Chaucer Review* 7 (1972), argues the opposite point of view: "Boccaccio . . . presents what he regards as a perfect affair, and its salient feature is that very sensuousness which love *paramours* affords and marriage cannot" (1). Janet Smarr, in *Boccaccio and Fiammetta: The Narrator as Lover* (Urbana: University of Illinois Press, 1986), while not accepting a view as extreme as ap Roberts's, argues that "Hollander tends to explain *away* the erotic aspects of Boccaccio's fictions in order to focus on their moral meanings; while these meanings are there and Hollander's book is important in pointing them out, nonetheless the dominant effect of these fictions seems to me precisely the doubleness of aspect, the attempt to join the erotic with the moral" (7).

13 In Agamemnon's refusal to return Criseis to her father, the precipitating event of the *Iliad,* Homer recalls the theft of Helen. Boccaccio's theme appears to be that such a crime is particularly characteristic of Troy, Homer's, that Greeks and Trojans alike are susceptible to it.

14 William S. Anderson, *The Art of the Aeneid* (Englewood Cliffs, NJ: Prentice-Hall, 1969), 100. Michael C. J. Putnam, in *The Poetry of the Aeneid* (Cambridge: Harvard University Press, 1966), suggests that Aeneas's wrathful slaying of Turnus is a victory for the irrational forces Juno has represented in the poem (200–201). J. William Hunt, *Forms of Glory* (Carbondale: Southern Illinois University Press, 1973), concurs: "It will always be possible to say that for Aeneas to have spared Turnus might have been a betrayal of his mission for which everything else had been endured, or that his taking of Turnus' life was an act of stark revenge culminating a series of disasters to friend and foe alike" (96). Williams observes of Turnus's submission, described by the word "humilis" in *Aeneid* 12.930, "Thus is the proud Turnus brought low. It was the purpose of Rome *debellare superbos* (6.853); that purpose has now in this instance been achieved, and the reader may expect Rome's mercy to come into play (*parcere subiectis*)" (*Aen.* 2:507 n. 930). For a brief survey of criticism on the killing of Turnus, see Williams, ibid., 2:502–3 n. 887f.

15 In the goddess Venus Boccaccio finds a powerful symbol that unites the themes of moral choice and divine influence and at the same time ties his poem to the *Aeneid.* As Robert Hollander has shown, Boccaccio's early works are frequently focused on a double figure of Venus. He observes, however, that "the *Filostrato* is the least classicizing of Boccaccio's early works. Yet even here Venus, the goddess of carnal love, if not a major 'character' in the work, is a major presence. Against her is posed no better

version of herself" (*Boccaccio's Two Venuses,* 52). This reading appears to overlook the celestial Venus Troilus describes in his hymn (see below).

16 In the *Aeneid* the gods are independent forces who frequently dominate the poem's action. In the *Filostrato* they are seen only in association with men, as if they were to be understood there primarily as aspects of human psychology. The gods reveal their intentions to men in the *Aeneid* in a variety of ways, but they act on Aeneas primarily through epiphanies and dreams. Venus appears to her son in *Aeneid* 1.313–410; Mercury appears to him in *Aeneid* 4.265–78. More commonly, Aeneas has dreams in which the will of some divinity is revealed to him: the dream of Hector (*Aen.* 2.268–97); the dream of the Lares and Penates (*Aen.* 3.147–75); the dream of Mercury, which follows the epiphany that he has not sufficiently heeded (*Aen.* 4.556–70). There are several others.

17 See Philip R. Hardie, *Virgil's Aeneid: Cosmos and Imperium* (Oxford: Clarendon Press, 1986), 5–85. W. R. Johnson counsels, however, that "Vergil seems to go out of his way to demonstrate the perils and confusion of the religious traditions from which such a theodicy might be fashioned" (*Darkness Visible: A Study of Vergil's "Aeneid"* [Berkeley: University of California Press, 1972], 142).

18 On this hymn, see Peter Dronke, "L'Amor che move il sole e l'altre stelle," *Studi medievali* 3d ser., vol. 6, fasc. 1 (1965): 389–423; Hollander, *Boccaccio's Two Venuses,* 177–79 nn. 100–105; James H. McGregor, "Troilus's Hymn to Venus and His Choice of Loves in Boccaccio's *Filostrato,*" *Romance Philology* 41 (1987): 48–57.

19 In addition to the works cited above, see Janet Smarr, "Boccaccio and the Choice of Hercules," *Modern Language Notes* 92 (1977): 146–52. Although she does not discuss this episode, her argument is nevertheless relevant to it.

20 Hollander argues that the final ten stanzas of the poem, "while continuing the religious language of the earlier stanzas, . . . make it plain that Troilo's interests are exclusively carnal"; he concludes, "Troilus is not asking to share any of the celestial gifts of *Venus Caelestis*" (*Boccaccio's Two Venuses,* 178 n. 101).

21 Venus does not govern above the third sphere, and the poem can tell us nothing of the universe beyond her.

3 *Filocolo*

1 Salvatore Battaglia, "Schemi lirici nell'arte del Boccaccio," *Archivum Romanicum* 19 (1935): 63–68. Although written more than fifty years ago, this article still serves as the starting point of modern assessments of Boccaccio. Battaglia asserts, "Il *Filocolo* è la prima opera del Boccaccio; pensata e stesa dallo scrittore non ancora ventiquattrenne, porta i segni dell'esuberanza giovanile, che non ha saputo ancora disciplinare la propria cultura e non riesce a infrenare la passionalità che gli urge nel petto; ma complessivamente, per il suo stesso disordine costruttivo che lo fa sconfinare a ogni passo dai limiti del romanzo, l'artista porta alla luce per la prima volta e con indiscriminato fervore tutti quei fermenti sentimentali e letterari che si affaciavano

alla sua coscienza: parecchi cadranno, quelli specialmente di derivazione troppo libresca; molti altri, e i più, ritorneranno con discrete variazioni nelle opere successive, mentre alcuni in forma più scaltrita giungeranno fino al *Decameron*. Ma per intendere nella loro vera prospettiva gli elementi che confluiscono nel *Filocolo*, è necessario riportarli al tono che domina in tutta l'opera e che si rivela d'indole essenzialmente sentimentale, più lirica che narrativa, rivolta a interessi passionali e più propriamente psicologici anziché a quelli romanzeschi con cui è stata concepita l'azione generale e a cui l'autore fa a tratti qualche larga concessione" (63). Nicholas J. Perella, in "The World of Boccaccio's *Filocolo*," *PMLA* 76 (1961): 330–39, concurs: "The vision of a refined and sublime secular life centered in the chivalric-courtly ideal (with its own center in love of woman), is the major inspirational motif in Boccaccio's literary career" (338). Even though Battaglia's major contention—that *Filocolo* is "more lyrical than narrative"—has been opposed, Victoria Kirkham, in "Reckoning with Boccaccio's *Questioni d'Amore*," *Modern Language Notes* 89 (1974): 47–59, concludes, "If we read the *Filocolo* as a substantially new version of the source tale, altered and expanded in order to accommodate the added dimension of Christian ethics, it does indeed display a design of narrative unity. By our standards the design is a failure because it seems so alien to the story at hand" (59).

Janet Smarr, in "Boccaccio's *Filocolo:* Romance Epic and Religious Allegory," *Forum Italicium* 12 (1978): 26–43, is alone in suggesting a single theme unifying the plot and rhetoric of *Filocolo*. She argues, "If Lelius' acceptance of the new faith illustrates not only an individual conversion but also the historical conversion of the pagan world, the Roman empire, and if the completion of his pilgrimage by Florio and Biancifiore and their large scale conversion of others illustrates the ultimate triumph of the church in the world, such a theme would justify Boccaccio's expansion of a romance into a lengthy prose epic with classical epic trappings" (41). While I disagree with Smarr's notion that the conversion of the kingdom of Florio represents an "ultimate" triumph of the church, I am, as this chapter shows, in absolute agreement with her belief that conversion plays a central role in the text.

2 See *Filoc.* 821–22 n. 10. Not Attila but Totila destroyed Florence in A.D. 542. Hans Baron, in *Crisis of the Early Italian Renaissance* (Princeton: Princeton University Press, 1966), notes the confusion about the two conquerors and observes the role this legend played in the politics of Boccaccio's period (97–98).

3 *Filoc.* 958 n. 6.

4 Ibid., 1.1.24, 3.20.21, 3.24.9.

5 The action of *Filocolo* 1.30–34 centers in Seville; Cordova is mentioned in *Filocolo* 5.88–95 passim.

6 On this name, "civitas marmorea," which Quaglio (*Filoc.* 729 n. 2) records as common in medieval chronicles, see Virginio Bertolini, "Dalla 'Marmorina' del Boccaccio all'appellativo di città marmorea dato a Verona nel medioevo," *Atti e memorie della Accademia di agricultura, scienze e lettere di Verona* 18 (1966–67): 321–32.

7 Ilario defines Florio, alias Filocolo, as "idolatrio . . . della setta de' gen-

tili" (*Filoc.* 5.52.7) and describes such men as subject to Roman suspicion as political enemies.

8 For a contemporary survey of the political situation of the late fifth to middle sixth centuries, see Giovanni Villani, *Cronica,* ed. Franco Gherardi Dragomanni (Florence, 1844; Frankfurt: Minerva, 1969), 2, 4.

9 Felice is described as "reggitore de' regni di Speria, nipote di Atalante" (*Filoc.* 1.10.1). Hesperia means the "Western land"; it is the name Vergil often uses for Italy (*Aen.* 1.53, 3.163, etc.). Boccaccio glosses it as Spain at *Tes.* 10.89.3.

10 See Vatican Mythographer (hereafter cited as Vat. Myth.) I: 183; Vat. Myth II: 33, 53. *In scriptores rerum mythicarum Latini tres.,* ed. G. H. Bode (Cellis: Schulze, 1834). Descent from Atlas also links Aeneas and Evander, and Aeneas insists on it (*Aen.* 8.140–41).

11 After crossing the Rubicon in 49 B.C., Caesar turned aside from the pursuit of Pompey's main force and battled against a smaller segment of it, which he defeated at Ilerda (Lerida) in that year. Augustus made himself permanent governor of Gaul and Spain.

12 Arabs are mentioned in *Filocolo* 1.26.25, 1.32.8.

13 *Filocolo* 1.26.5 describes the arrows of Felice's soldiers as "gittate dagli archi di Partia dalle arabe braccia."

14 *Paulus Orosius historiarum adversum paganos libri septem,* ed. Adolf Lippold, Fond. Lorenzo Valla, Scrittori Greci e Latini (Milan: Mondadori, 1976). (All Orosius quotations are from this edition.) Orosius sees this as a decisive moment in Roman history. The birth of Christ, he says, occurs "anno imperii Caesaris quadragesimo secundo, cum facta pace cum Parthis Iani portae clausae sunt et bella toto orbe cessarunt" (1.1.6).

15 See above, n. 6.

16 As I have described above, n. 10, his descent from Atlas links him with Aeneas. As his conversion at the end of the text implies, Felice is not an absolute antagonist of *Romanitas* and Roman Christianity. These Trojan identifications, in the peculiar language of the text, prepare for his conversion.

17 Orosius 6.1.6–8, 6.17.10, 6.22.4, 6.22.8, and especially 6.20.5–9.

18 Ibid., 6.20.4.

19 Janet Smarr observes that "Boccaccio's reason for choosing Scipio Africanus [as ancestor for Biancifiore] probably comes from Dante's use of the Roman hero; for Dante mentions him in all three parts of the *Commedia* as well as in other writings" ("Boccaccio's *Filocolo,*" 40).

20 See Orosius 7.1.1.

21 MS Florence, National Library, B.R. 50.

22 Aldo Maria Constantini, in "Studi sullo *Zibaldone Magliabechiano,*" *Studi sul Boccaccio* 7 (1973), describes the contents of folios 20r–83r: "Compendio di storia imperiale, dalla caduta della repubblica romana alla morte di Federico II. Il lungo trattato storico (divisible in due parti: una prima si conclude con Onorio—là dove termina l'opera di Paolo Orosio—al f. 75r., la seconda si apre con Teodosio II e si basa sulla cronaca di Martino Polono che ne costituisce l'unica fonte) si avvale delle opere di Cesare, Suetonio,

pseudo-Egesippo, Eusebio, Eutropio, Orosio e, come già detto, Martino Polono; ma è probabile che il lavoro di ricerca delle fonti e costruzione del racconto sia stato fatto da uno storico medievale che il Boccaccio ha trascritto" (27).

In *Paradiso* 6, the canto from which Boccaccio apparently took his information about Justinian (see *Filoc.* 958 n. 6), Dante presents a similar view of Rome's providential history and centers on the men and events Boccaccio and Orosius highlight: the Scipios, Julius and Augustus, and, of course, Justinian himself.

23 Dido is described as "pattorita," that is, "contracted," as in marriage (*Filoc.* 1.1.1). This reading, which Quaglio prefers (*Filoc.* 713 n. 2), makes considerable sense given the emphasis on marriage in *Filocolo.*

24 As Janet Smarr remarks, "The book opens with echoes of the *Aeneid* as Juno once again plots to overcome the Trojans who have settled in Italy. This time Jove consents to their defeat" ("Boccaccio's *Filocolo,*" 26).

25 Juno's evocation of Allecto is described in *Aeneid* 7.323–405.

26 A very indirect precedent is suggested by the description in *Aeneid* 8.319–29 of Saturn's founding of Latium. After being supplanted as chief Olympian by his son, Jupiter, Saturn founds the Latin kingdom on principles that have been essentially outmoded by the Jovian accession to power. It is not until Aeneas brings Trojan (and Jovian) culture to them that their retrograde identity is overcome.

27 Aenas prays for a cessation of his "Troiana . . . fortuna" in *Aeneid* 6.62.

28 Lust such as that implied by sacrifice to Priapus (*Filoc.* 1.1.7) and characteristic of these "Trojans" is not seen as fruitful in the allegory of this passage.

29 Rom. 9:7–8, Douay-Confraternity translation.

30 As I have already noted, Felice's kingdom is first presented through reminiscences of *Aeneid* 2. In yielding to the suggestions of the satanic messenger and interpreting the bull prodigy, Felice is acting like Priam. Thus his kingdom represents Troy on the brink of its divinely sanctioned destruction.

31 Jupiter says to Venus that, to the Romans, "ego nec metas rerum nec tempora pono: / imperium sine fine dedi" (*Aen.* 1.278).

32 The pageant of Aeneas's "children" in *Aeneid* 6.752–853 and the shield of Aeneas in *Aeneid* 8.608–731 reveal the historical effect of Aeneas' conquest of Italy.

33 This use of paganism as an image of heresy accounts for the fact that, throughout *Filocolo,* pagan and Christian themes are treated in the same classicizing language.

34 Pluto, like Sinon, acts only to destroy. His aim is interruption of the pilgrimage to Spain, "che lo essercizio era alle sue invasioni inique contrario" (*Filoc.* 1.9.1). He does not realize that his act will bring about the very opposite of what he plans, for with the eventual conversion of Felice's kingdom new Christians are made and the opening of the pilgrimage road is guaranteed.

35 Images of pregnancy are frequently repeated in Vergil's descriptions of the Trojan horse (*Aen.* 2.20, 2.38, 2.52, 2.238, etc.).

36 *Filoc.* 752 n. 10. Robert Hollander remarks, "If the *Ars amatoria* is to be their moral guide, we may expect them to fall passionately in love" (*Boccaccio's Two Venuses,* 32).

On the complex problem of reading the *Ars amatoria,* see Hollander's summary argument, *Boccaccio's Two Venuses,* 115–16. Janet Smarr notes, "Florio and Biancifiore fell in love over the *Ars amatoria* like Paolo and Francesca over the story of Lancelot" ("Boccaccio's *Filocolo,*" 37). On the *Ars amatoria* as a schoolbook in the Middle Ages, see James H. McGregor, "Ovid at School from the Ninth to the Fourteenth Centuries," *Classical Folia* 32 (1978): 29–42.

37 *Filocolo* 1.45.2 describes "Citerea, donna del loro ascendente." For the role of astrology in *Filocolo,* see A. E. Quaglio, *Scienza e mito nel primo Boccaccio* (Padua: Liviana, 1967).

38 As undisciplined, unaided, and endangered lovers, Florio and Biancifiore often resemble Pyramus and Thisbe; see especially *Filocolo* 2.21.

39 "Frater ut Aeneas pelago tuus omnia circum / litora iactetur odiis Iunonis acerbae, / nota tibi, et nostro doluisti saepe dolore. / nunc Phoenissa tenet Dido blandisque moratur / vocibus, et vereor quo se Iunonia vertant hospitia" (*Aen.* 1.667–72).

40 Hollander sees in this reference "to the inflammation of Dido . . . anti-Roman (and for a medieval reader anti-Christian) overtones" (*Boccaccio's Two Venuses,* 32). Smarr apparently concurs in this negative view of Venus's actions: "The parallel to Dido's enamorment in the *Aeneid* provides us with another connection among the epic, romance, and religious elements of the work. For as the goddesses' plot in Vergil's text was intended to keep Aeneas from his divinely appointed mission of establishing Rome, we can see in this an analogy to Satan's temporarily successful interruption of the pilgrimage in Book 1. Here, after all, the Romans have become Christians. It is similarly the deceit of Venus which interrupts the course of life for the two youngsters. For it is because Florio and Biancifiore ignore the worship of Diana that they are troubled and parted by the slighted deity" ("Boccaccio's *Filocolo,*" 28). Neither Hollander nor Smarr seems to be reading the *Aeneid* straightforwardly. Venus's purpose in the *Aeneid* is to destroy Dido and Carthage, because she feels they threaten Rome and Aeneas. Her pact with Juno, whom she mistrusts, is made with this aim. In *Filocolo,* Biancifiore, the Roman, is to be used, as Aeneas is used, to destroy the kingdom of Felice (although, of course, that "destruction" will be ultimate salvation). Biancifiore is the opposite of the satanic messenger who acts against the Roman pilgrims. She carries out the same providential task in the end, however, since Pluto acts unwittingly (as Satan always must in Christian orthodoxy) to aid the very Christians he despises. Ironically, too, Aeneas, not unlike Sinon, destroys a kingdom that offers him shelter and compassion.

41 Venus uses love; she even injects the lovers with "segreto veleno" (*Filoc.* 2.2.5), but she does not oppose them as she does Dido. However, her means are crude and carry with them dangerous side effects.

42 Felice, who knows Biancifiore's illustrious ancestry, begins from this point

to deny it. He describes her as "una romana popolaresca femina, non conosciuta e nutricata nelle nostre case come una serva" (ibid., 2.7.10).

43 The impossibility is also given an astrological explanation in ibid., 2.9.2: "Venus era nell'auge del suo epiciclo," and this makes her influence irresistible.

44 Ibid., 2.33.10. This plot eventually works to the king's disadvantage, for during the ceremonial presentation, Biancifiore is entitled to ask for and receives the king's consent to her marriage to Florio (ibid., 2.35.6).

45 Felice is the descendant of Atlas, leader of the Titans.

46 This Venus resembles "the philosophical Venus in Alan of Lille's *De planctu naturae.* The chaste Venus married to Hymen is the mother of Cupid, who represents appetite moderated by reason" (Earl G. Schreiber, "Venus in the Medieval Mythographic Tradition," *Journal of English and Germanic Philology* 74 [1975]: 532).

47 *Anicii Manlii Severini Boethii Philosophiae Consolatio,* ed. Ludwig Beiler, CCL 94 (Turnholt: Brepols, 1957), 1.1.1–6 (hereafter cited as *Phil. Cons.*).

48 Philosophy notes that she and Boethius are accused together (ibid., 1.5.9).

49 "Venere intenta a' suoi suggetti, comosse il cielo e per loro porse pietosi prieghi a Giove, col consentimento del quale e di ciascuno altro iddio, il necessario aiuto si dispose a porgere" (*Filoc.* 4.134.1).

Both Robert Hollander (*Boccaccio's Two Venuses,* 33–34) and Janet Smarr ("Boccaccio's *Filocolo,*" 36) emphasize the role of Diana in separating the lovers and her inclusion in the love's marriage and reunion. Hollander argues that after a slight to Diana (*Filoc.* 3. 24. 1), "the restoration of each lover to each is now apparently impossible under the aegis of Venus alone" (34). I have emphasized the degree of cooperation Venus elicits among the gods and her own eclectic and philosophical nature in the iconography and action of *Filocolo.*

50 "The *Filocolo* also celebrates marriage as the human relation that can accommodate human love by reconciling chastity with natural desires" (Smarr, "Boccaccio's *Filocolo,*" 37).

51 *Filocolo* 5.63.4 reveals that the love of Florio and Biancifiore was the will not just of the pagan gods but of God himself.

52 Janet Smarr argues, "We are in a Spenser-like allegory of projected emotions and states of mind. The proper service to the gods in this context is the proper maintenance of their virtues. In such a scheme divine intervention might logically cease when humans reach a state of virtuous equilibrium which marriage is in Boccaccio's view" ("Boccaccio's *Filocolo,*" 28). Smarr's emphasis here does not work against the historical function of the deities in *Filocolo* but complements it by an allegorical reading.

53 It is suggested that Florio's conversion will return his father's kingdom to Roman control, "come già fu" (*Filoc.* 5.68).

54 Janet Smarr speaks of the intersection of two plots in the text: "The horizontal Ovidian narrative about young human lovers is paired with the vertical story of Christ's incarnation and redemption of man" ("Boccaccio's *Filocolo,*" 34). I see the vertical plot as including all the providential events in the history of the Roman Empire and Christianity, an axis that includes

the Incarnation. Florio and Biancifiore illustrate the way individual love becomes a historical force.

55 Orosius, 6.1.19–20.

4 *Teseida* 1

1 Alberto Limentani identifies "due fulcri, due nodi d'interesse contenutistico e d'esperienza costruttiva e linguistica: quello delle armi e quello dell'amore, appunto. Ma il singolare eclettismo del poeta, la sua tecnica contaminatoria, potremmo dire il suo 'trasformismo,' tendono a indebolire e scalzare i due perni, che oscillano di continuo" (*Tes.* 233).

2 Giuseppe Velli ("L'apoteosi di Arcita: Ideologia e coscienza storica nel *Teseida,*" *Studi e Problemi di Critica Testuale* 5 [1972]: 33–66, now in *Petrarca e Boccaccio: Tradizione, Memoria, Scrittura. Studi sul Petrarca* 7. [Padua: Antenore, 1979], 150–52) is virtually alone in crediting Boccaccio with the kind of response to the antique I have been describing. In *Teseida,* he argues, "I riferimenti classici, è facile rendersene conto, non sono disposti secondo linee casuali, centrifughe, non sono solo attributi esteriori volti a dare alla vicenda, mediante l'allontanamento nel tempo ed una esotica collocazione geografica, carattere di favolosa. . . . Resta imponente, lo sforzo di restituzione" (151). It is more common to see Boccaccio's classicizing as best represented not by the poem but by the poet's glosses to *Teseida.* On these glosses, see Alberto Limentani, "Tendenze della prosa del Boccaccio ai margini del *Teseida,*" *Giornale storico della letteratura italiana* 135 (1958): 524–51; Robert Hollander, "The Validity of Boccaccio's Self-Exegesis in His *Teseida,*" *Medievalia et humanistica* n.s. 8 (1977): 163–84; and Piero Boitani, *Chaucer and Boccaccio,* 20–31.

3 Vittore Branca concludes, "In the whole period of his literary apprenticeship at Naples, Boccaccio did not succeed in going beyond the schemes of the literature of romantic chivalry" ("Myth of the Hero," 268).

4 Robert Hollander argues, "If the *Filostrato* displayed some of Boccaccio's eagerness to win repute as the Italian inheritor of the epic tradition, the *Teseida* is the result of some fairly feverish labor in that direction. Still, despite the frequent imitation of Vergil and Statius (especially the latter) and the 'martial' nature of Books I, II, and VIII, it is the romantic elements which predominate heavily; one can sense Boccaccio's ease and comfort when he leaves the battles of Book II for the amorous 'battles' of Book III. For here, as elsewhere, his great *materia* is love (*Boccaccio's Two Venuses,* 53). Branca sees the poem as Boccaccio's triumph over himself: "Per la prima volta il tumultuoso autobiografismo sentimentale è raccolto e frenato dall'arte" (*Profilo,* 50).

5 Branca begins by calling it a "decisively epical poem," but he then repeats earlier judgments of its imperfections ("Myth of the Hero," 270). Limentani makes this reference the starting point of his analysis of the poem, but he too rejects Boccaccio's claim (*Tes.* 232). See above, n. 1.

6 *Thebaid* 12, the epic's final book, contains the same materials as the Creon

episode of *Teseida* 2, with the very important exception that Statius provides no Palemone and Arcita for Theseus to contend with. On the final book of *Thebaid* (*Theb.*) and the godlike Theseus, see below and David Vessey, *Statius and Thebaid*, (Cambridge: Cambridge University Press, 1973), 307–16.

7 This has not been observed by critics of *Teseida*. On the name "Emilia," see G. Billanovich, *Restauri Boccacceschi* (Rome: Edizioni di Storia e Letteratura, 1947), 121 n. 1.

8 Aeneas is recognized by Latinus as Lavinia's destined bridegroom (*Aen.* 7.255–59). By the terms of the duel (*Aen.* 12.192–94), he lays claim to her again.

9 Hollander observes, "What is most impressive about the love sponsored by Venus and Cupid here is that it acts upon the previously chaste in such a way that marriage is an immediate result. [Venus] is . . . celestial in her provenance" (*Boccaccio's Two Venuses,* 53).

10 Limentani notes the Vergilian source (*Tes.* 889 n. 9). In his introduction, however, he concludes, "Da Virgilio il Boccaccio ha tratto poco" (237).

11 Boccaccio summarizes the war in two octaves (*Tes.* 2.10–11 and a gloss *ad Tes.* 2.10).

12 Limentani notes that "la morte di Creonte . . . come larga parte del secondo libro è improntata al dodicesimo di Stazio: ma è innegabile che gli ultimi istanti del guerriero e lo sciogliersi dell'anima dal corpo contengano un ricordo chiaro delle analoghe figurazioni dell'*Eneide*" (*Tes.* 238).

13 *Clementia* is an imperial virtue as well as one common to all men. Vessey observes that, in his progress to the temple of Clementia, Theseus, as he is in Boccaccio, is "depicted as a Roman triumphator" (*Statius and Thebaid,* 312 n. 2). Stefan Weinstock, in *Divus Julius* (Oxford: Clarendon Press, 1971), 233–43, associates decisive changes in the use of the Latin word with Caesar and with Cicero writing about Caesar. Vessey argues, "In Theseus, Statius portrays the model of a clement and just king, worthy to rule over the city which is the home of Clementia. . . . In the *Thebaid,* the Amazons . . . serve to represent societies governed by lawless and primitive violence" (312).

14 Venus's voice ("nec vox hominem sonat") and her face ("haud tibi vultus / mortalis") (*Aen.* 1.326–27) give her away. Emilia has an "angelica voce" (*Tes.* 3.10.8); when Arcita is admiring her, "nel viso" (*Tes.* 3.12.7), he is moved to proclaim her heavenly nature.

15 On the use and abuse of love, or *caritas* and *concupiscentia*, see Saint Augustine, *On Christian Doctrine* (1:29), where he suggests that true love can be shared as the enthusiasm for an actor is joyfully shared by his fans. Carnal love, however, cannot be.

16 "Once we enter the third book we re-enter a familiar world: the sweet springtime of Venus and her son with all its painful consequence" (Hollander, *Boccaccio's Two Venuses,* 54).

17 The love that Theseus feels can be distinguished in an ironic way from the love that the Thebans feel. So far, Palemone and Arcita are blissful in their love for the heavenly Emilia. Theseus, however, when he first sees Hippolyta, is excited and "lieto aspetta / d'avere in braccio quella stella chiara"

(*Tes.* 1.131.5–6). Marriage gives expression to his desire, but Palemone and Arcita struggle to find an expression for a passion that becomes increasingly like Theseus's.

18 Egli era bello, e d'alberi novelli
tutto fronzuto e di nova verdura;
e era lieto di canti d'uccelli,
di chiare fonti fresche a dismisura,
che sopra l'erbe facevan ruscelli
freddi e nemici d'ogni gran calura;
conigli, lepri, cervi e cavriuoli
vi si prendean con cani e con lacciuoli. (*Tes.* 4.65)

On this bosk, see Giorgio Barberi Squarotti, *Fine dell'idillio* (Genoa: Il Melangolo, 1978), 269–70. On the *locus amoenus* in general, see E. R. Curtius, *European Literature and the Latin Middle Ages,* trans. Willard R. Trask (New York: Harper and Row, 1953), 190–202; A. Bartlett Giamatti, *The Earthly Paradise and the Renaissance Epic* (Princeton: Princeton University Press, 1966), 11–94, especially 15–33. Some elements of this garden, particularly the rabbits and the snares, strongly suggest the garden of earthly delight, "where Cupid operates. It has been tainted by Cupid ever since the Fall, when cupidity gained ascendency over the reason" (D. W. Robertson, Jr., *Preface to Chaucer* [Princeton: Princeton University Press, 1965], 95). A strictly Robertsonian reading of the garden is not wise. Since Boccaccio carefully describes the deterioration of the bosk through the triumph of *furor* and finally death, it is unnecessary to project into the first image, when the bosk is still uncorrupted by man's libido, an image of its final destruction. The source of that final destruction—the fire of love—is at this point only threatening.

19 The implication of the landscape in the *furor* of war is an appropriate theme for a poem in which Palemone and Arcita will soon be portrayed as Aeneas and Turnus fighting for the love of Lavinia. In the *Thebaid,* too, there is a similar involvement of the landscape of Nemea in the *furor* of the Argive forces. See Vessey, *Statius and Thebaid,* 165–67.

20 *Aen.* 12.176–211. See also McGregor, *Image of Antiquity,* chap. 4.

21 William S. Anderson observes, "On [Juno's] side Vergil places anger and the other passions, irrational thinking and action, destructivity of others and self" (*Art of the Aeneid,* 13).

22 Michael Putnam sees a deep irony in Turnus's death: "It should cause little wonder when Juno seems to surrender so readily to Jupiter's plea that she give over her anger in contemplation of future Roman magnificence. For, according to the poet's wishes, it is she, not Aeneas, nor the grandeur for which Augustus seems to stand, who wins the greatest victory as the soul of Turnus passes with a resentful moan to the shades below" (*Poetry of the Aeneid,* 201).

23 Without Boccaccio's gloss defining Priapus as "dio degli orti" (*ad Tes.* 5.62.2), we would probably associate him with the negative iconography of fruitless lust that is linked to him in *Filocolo* 1.1.7.

24 Putnam argues, "Turnus stands . . . for Italy and consequently absorbs into

himself for the final clash all the challenge of Mezentius and Aeneas' other foes, all the pastoral freedom of Camilla, the heroine of Book XI, as he begins the last attempt to oppose destiny against insuperable odds" (*Poetry of the "Aeneid,"* 151).

25 Limentani refers to several uses of the dragon simile in the popular romance *Febus* (*Tes.* 894 n. 22). It is equally likely, however, that Thebans fighting in a grove should recall the dragon from whose teeth this race was bred.

26 Limentani sees this scene in which Emilia takes part as "una vera e propria scena trecentesca di caccia col falcone" (ibid., 894 n. 22).

27 "Rapì Teseo nella sua giovanezza Elena, figliuola di Tindaro, la quale fu poi rapita da Paris; ma la madre di Teseo la rendé a Castore e a Polluce, suoi fratelli, senza essere ella stata tocca da Teseo: per che gli fu cotale ingiuria perdonata" (*ad Tes.* 5.92.5–6).

28 *Thebaid* (*P. Papini Stati Thebais,* ed. Alfred Klotz and T. C. Klinnert [Leipzig: Teubner, 1973]) 4.32–308. See also Vessey, *Statius and Thebaid,* 196–205; *Aen.* 7.647–817.

29 On the analogy between the games in *Aeneia* 5 and the war in Italy and also the games in *Thebaid* 6 and the war at Thebes, see Vessey, *Statius and Thebaid,* 209–29.

30 Turnus (*Aen.* 9.123–75) describes a supposed equivalence between Helen and Lavinia, the Trojan camp and walled Troy, himself and the conquering Greeks. Anderson calls Turnus's view a "misinterpretation" (*Aen.* 77).

31 These champions are involved in the chariot race described in *Thebaid* 6.389–549.

32 Vessey, *Statius and Thebaid,* 198–99.

33 Ibid., 199.

34
> Sed regna Tyri germanus habebat
> Pygmalion, scelere ante alios immanior omnis.
> quos inter medius venit furor, ille Sychaeum
> impius ante aras atque auri caecus amore
> clam ferro incautum superat, securus amorum
> germanae. (*Aen.* 1.346–51)

35 McGregor, "Theater of Theseus," 1–42.

36 McGregor, *Image of Antiquity,* chap. 4.

37 Hollander, *Boccaccio's Two Venuses,* 55–65, is the most complete.

38 *Tes.* 896 n. 27.

39 Putnam describes a reversal of roles by Aeneas, "forced by circumstances to adopt a position not unlike that of Turnus himself in Book XII or the Greeks in II, where violence, even needless violence, is created to attain an end" (*Poetry of the Aeneid,* 152).

40 *Tes.* 896 n. 7.

41 The source of this episode is *Thebaid* 6.485–90, as Limentani observes (*Tes.* 897 n. 25). Horses appear to represent the bestial aspects of the men who ride them. Thus Palemone is seized by a horse, not overcome by a man, and Arcita is crushed in a fall from a horse. Although this equation of passion and mount is common in Christian allegory, it is also present in Statius. In the horse race described in *Thebaid* 6, Polynices is overpowered by his

horse; as Vessey notes, "Polynices cannot rule the horse any more than he can govern his own destiny" (*Statius and Thebiad,* 215).

42 Limentani notes that this scene loosely recalls *Aeneid* 10.755–68, where the gods look down on the Italian battlefield and especially on the doomed Mezentius, the figure Arcita, in the fall from his horse, most resembles (*Tes.* 897 n. 27).

43 Limentani sees the Tisiphone episode in *Thebaid* 8.342–47 as crucial here (*Tes.* 897 n. 4). Tisiphone is closely modeled on Vergil's Allecto, as Vessey notes (*Statius and Thebaid,* 75). See also Walter Pabst, *Venus als Heilige und Furie in Boccaccios Fiammetta-Dichtung* (Krefeld: Scherpe, 1958).

44 Putnam recalls "many references in Book XII associating Turnus with Dido" (*Poetry of the Aeneid,* 198).

45 The following paragraphs summarize part of my argument in "Theater of Theseus."

46 *Isidori Hispalensis Episcopi Etymologiarum sive Originum libri XX (Etym.),* ed. W. M. Lindsay (Oxford: Clarendon Press, 1911), 18, 52.

5 *Teseida* 2

1 Limentani details, in a summary table, correspondences between passages in *Teseida* 11 and in *Thebaid* 6 (*Tes.* 898 n. 3). See also Alberto Limentani, "Boccaccio 'traduttore' di Stazio," *La Rassegna* 64 (1960): 237–40.

2 *Tes.* 2.78–80, 10.3–8.

3 The tree felling is executed in *Teseida* 11.18–26. It reflects both Statius's account in *Thebaid* 6.90–107 and Ovid's in *Metamorphoses* (*Ovidii Nasonis Metamorphoses,* ed. William S. Anderson [Leipzig: Teubner, 1977]) 8.739–79. Tree-felling episodes are *topoi* in classical poetry; see Gordon Williams, *Tradition and Originality in Roman Poetry* (Oxford: Clarendon Press, 1968), 263.

4 For examples, see Horace, *Epistles* 2.2.72–75 and *Satires* 1.6.42–44.

5 On accusations as a motif of ancient mourning, see Richmond Lattimore, *Themes in Greek and Latin Epitaphs* (Urbana: University of Illinois Press, 1962), 153.

6 Limentani has remarked that Boccaccio gives the crowd a more important role to play in *Teseida* than the one it plays in *Thebaid:* "L'elemento più cospicuo nella resa boccacciana è dato dal ruolo che viene ad assumere la cornice della folla; laddove in Stazio essa resta di sfondo, e campeggiano le manifestazioni dolorose di re Licurgo e specie della madre, nel *Teseida* questa disperazione si inquadra in un contorno più vivo e marcato, per il quale sono fin troppo ovvi i richiami a certe pitture del tempo . . . o, più direttamente, alle sacre rappresentazioni, o, ancor meglio, in campo profano agli stessi cantari" ("Boccaccio 'traduttore,'" 238). Limentani's recourse to a period and stylistic explanation of this phenomenon is certainly reasonable. It does not, however, address the thematic purpose of the scene.

7 Limentani sees Boccaccio as introducing "un accento più esagitato" in his imitation of Statius: "Mentre Licurgo offre al rogo una ciocca di capelli,

Palemone 's'avea / la barba e' crin tutti quanti tagliati,' e anziche *fletu pio,* parla 'con sommo pianto'; e prima a Licurgo, *exutus honore vittarum,* sta di fronte un 'Palemone di lugubre manto / coperto' " (ibid., 239). It is incorrect, however, to see Boccaccio's transformations of Lycurgus's mourning in this way. The king cast more than a "ciocca di capelli" on the corpse: "Tergoque et pectore fusam / caesariem ferro minuit sectisque iacentes / obnubit tenuia ora comis" (*Theb.* 6.194–96). While Palemone's "sommo pianto" exaggerates the phrase *fletu pio,* Lycurgus is also referred to as *insanus,* and his inability to hear words of comfort is compared to the inability of the raging Ionian sea to hear a mariner's vows and cries (*Theb.* 6.51–53). Lycurgus, moreover, is not only "exutus honore vittarum," that is, without the badges of his ritual office as priest, but, continuing the same phrase, "sedet ipse exutus honore / vittarum nexu genitor squalentia ora / sparsus et incultam ferali pulvere barbam" (*Theb.* 6.30–32). Lycurgus's squalor, his rage, and his impiety are all understated by Boccaccio, not by any means exaggerated. The contrast Limentani wishes to make between classical decorum and medieval lack of restraint is certainly not supported by this passage.

8 Poi fé subitamente Palemone,
là dove il rogo d'Arcita era stato,
edificar con mira operazione
un tempio grande, bello e elevato,
il qual sacrò alla santa Giunone;
e in quel volle che 'l cener guardato
fosse d'Arcita. (*Tes.* 11.69.1–6)

Limentani refers to *Thebaid* 6.238–48 and *Aeneid* 1.446–93 (*Tes.* 899 n. 9).

9 On temple-tombs, see Jocelyn Toynbee, *Death and Burial in the Roman World* (London: Thames and Hudson, 1971), 130–32.

10 See König, *Begegnung im Tempel.*

11 Raynaud de Lage, "Les Romans antiques," 276.

12 On the games in Vergil and Statius, see Vessey, *Statius and Thebaid,* 209–29, and Putnam, *Poetry of the Aeneid,* 64–105.

13 *Aeneid* 5.315–39 and *Thebaid* 6.593–645 describe footraces, and in both poems the details of the races are memorable. In the *Aeneid,* Nisus slips in a pool of blood from a sacrificial victim and deliberately fouls his closest competitor so that his lover, Euryalus, can win the race. In *Thebaid,* Idas pulls the hair of the front-runner and the race is rerun.

14 *Aeneid* 5.340–61 describes the prize giving.

15 Ovid, *Met.* 6.1–145.

16 Vessey, *Statius and Thebaid,* 216.

17 On this figure in another of Boccaccio's early works, see Janet Smarr, "Boccaccio and the Choice of Hercules."

18 Ovid's Pallas begins her cloth with the same first scene (*Met.* 6.70–82).

19 "Primus omnium Jovem appellavit, simulacra reperit, aram statuit, victimas immolavit, nequaquam istiusmodi rebus in Graecia unquam visis" *Eusebii Pamphili Chronicorum liber secundus S. Hieronymo interprete et ampliatore,* ed. J. L. Migne, Pat. Lat. 27:231. See also *S. Aureli Augustini De Civitate*

Dei, ed. Bernard Dombart and Alphonse Kalb, CCL 48 (Turnholt: Brepols, 1955), 18.8–9.

20 Isidore of Seville characterizes him in the same way (*Etym.* 8.11.10).

21 Boccaccio's gloss here is quite similar to a passage in Augustine's *De Civitate Dei*, 18.8.

22 *P. Ovidii Nasonis Fastorum libri sex*, ed. J. B. Pighi (Turin: Paravia, 1973), 6.696.

23 For an excellent introduction to the role of music in patristic and medieval thought, see Robertson, *Preface to Chaucer*, 114–37.

24 "Itaque sine Musica nulla disciplina potest esse perfecta, nihil enim sine illa. Nam et ipse mundus quaedam harmonia sonorum fertur esse compositus, et caelum ipsud sub harmoniae modulatione revolvi. Musica movet affectus, provocat in diversum habitum sensus. In proeliis quoque tubae concentus pugnantes accendit, et quanto vehementior fuerit clangor, tanto fit ad certamen animus fortior. Siquidem et remiges cantus hortatur, ad tolerandos quoque labores musica animum mulcet, et singulorum operum fatigationem modulatio vocis solatur. Excitos quoque animos musica sedat, sicut de David legitur, qui ab spiritu inmundo Saulem arte modulationis eripuit. Ipsas quoque bestias, necnon et serpentes, volucres atque delphinas ad auditum suae modulationis musica provocat. Sed et quidquid loquimur, vel intrinsecus venarum pulsibus commovemur, per musicos rhythmos harmoniae virtutibus probatur esse sociatum" (Isidore, *Etym.*, 3.17).

25 "Because thou . . . has eaten of the tree, whereof I commanded thee that thou shouldst not eat, cursed is the earth in thy work; with labor and with toil shalt thou eat thereof all the days of thy life." (Gen. 3:17).

26 William S. Anderson, *Ovid's Metamorphoses, Books 6–10* (Norman: University of Oklahoma Press, 1972), 168.

27 According to Limentani, the source of this notion is *Paradiso* 27.148 (*Tes.* 899 n. 3).

28 For an excellent summary of the medieval view of fame and its origins, see B. G. Koonce, *Chaucer and the Tradition of Fame* (Princeton: Princeton University Press, 1978), 13–45.

29 Ibid., 37.

30 "All human glory [Petrarch] concludes is but snow to the sun before time" (ibid., 40). See also Aldo S. Bernardo, *Petrarch, Scipio and the Africa* (Baltimore: Johns Hopkins University Press, 1962), 64–67.

31 Koonce, *Chaucer and Fame*, 17.

Appendix

1 Glosses *ad Tes.* 7.4.8, 7.27.3.

2 Boccaccio's gloss explains a "palestral gioco": "Palestrale giuoco era che gli uomini si solevano sopra le carni vestire un cuio strettissimo e morbido, nel quale niuno altro pertugio si vedea se non per me' gli occhi, acciò che veder potesse, e per me' la bocca, acciò che potesse spirare; poi così vestiti s'ugnevano tutti o d'olio o di sevo, e quindi si prendevano a guisa

di coloro che fanno alle braccia; e era reputata gran forza e gran destreza quella di colui che alcuno altro poteva o mettere in terra o tener fermo. E in questo cotale giuoco entravano alcuna volta le donne; e Elena, anzi che fosse moglie di Menelao, essendo ancora pulcella, intrata in questo giuoco, come che molto chiusa fosse, pur fu conosciuta da Teseo e rapita da lui" (*ad Tes.* 7.4.8).

3 On the shield of Aeneas, see Williams's summary bibliography in *Aeneid* 2:265–66 n. 608f. Putnam sees the shield as emblematic of "violence ultimately leading to peace" (*Poetry of the Aeneid*, 147–50).

4 "Quello che cesto si sia non abbiamo oggi assai chiaro; ma credo io che sia uno bastone al quale siano appiccate palle di piombo, con le quali l'uno percuote l'altro di coloro che vi giuocano, e è pericoloso e mortal giuoco" (*ad Tes.* 11.64.1). The *caestus* is in fact a leather boxing glove sometimes weighted with lead. The word "caestus" can also mean a stick, and Boccaccio attempts to accommodate this meaning, too. The result is surprising, but it is equally surprising that, when reading the accounts in Vergil, *Aeneid* 5.387–484, or *Thebaid* 6.731–825, of the brutal contests at the *caestus,* one is not sharply reminded of its incorrectness.

5 *Filos.* 3.80. See also McGregor, "Troilus's Hymn to Venus."

6 Boccaccio does not describe the contest in the text, but he defines the game in a gloss: "Desco era una palla ritonda, la quale a quel tempo essi usavano di gittare e in pinta e in volta, come oggi si gittano le pietre" (*ad Tes.* 11.66.2).

7 Vergil, *Eclogues,* ed. Robert Coleman (Cambridge: Cambridge University Press, 1977), *Ecloga* 10.26–30.

8 It is unfortunate that we lack the gloss to this final allegory, for it would be an interesting one indeed. Boccaccio's reference to the "forma vera" of Pan is quite intriguing. It may suggest the epiphany of Pan described in this passage of the *Eclogues.* The shepherds emphasize that they saw him ("quem vidimus ipsi"); and his visage, as Michael Putnam describes it, "painted with the vermillion with which triumphant Roman heroes were colored, puts into relief the importance of the occasion" (*Virgil's Pastoral Art* [Princeton: Princeton University Press, 1970], 353–59). Boccaccio describes Minerva's changing of her disguise and her appearance in "forma vera." This expression Dante reserves for a very special place in his poetry. In the *Vita nuova* he describes Amor's mourning over the corpse of a young woman: "Audite quanto Amor le fece orranza / ch'io 'l vidi lamentare in forma vera / sovra la morta imagine avvenente" (8.6).

The *forma vera* contrasts with the *morta imagine.* Commentators have not hesitated to suggest that the true form of love for Dante is Beatrice. Is it in such a sense that we are to understand the *forma vera* of Pan? The *forma vera* of Minerva is her true image as a goddess. Amor's true form, however, is Beatrice. Boccaccio refers to Pan's appearance in "forma di pastore" and in his "vera forma" as if these were identical. The implication of this seems to be that his human form and divine manifestation are the same, or that this duality represents him as he is. In this way he may represent a deity incarnated as a shepherd. Christ, the Good Shepherd, is another of this sort. As Vergil defines him in another *Eclogue:* "Pan curat ovis oviumque magistros" (*Ecl.* 2.33). Such responsibilities too seem to suit him admirably to represent the Good Shepherd himself.

I think that Boccaccio is ultimately suggesting that Pan represents Christ. This would certainly make him an appropriate culmination of the emblems that emerge from the games at Arcita's death. Christ, moreover, is the only one who can finally answer the challenge posed by that death, for he promises to his worshipers the conquest of death. He is also, of course, the ultimate persuasion against the kind of love that misleads Arcita. His story is a counsel against such love. It is not possible and perhaps not desirable to be firm in this assertion. Pan may represent and prefigure Christ; he need not do so. The emblems that emerge from the games are complete without that identification.

Index